HOW TO DO
PRIVACY
IN THE 21ST
CENTURY

SQUINT

BOOKS FOR A BUSY WORLD

Look More Closely

HOW TO DO PRIVACY IN THE 21ST CENTURY

THE TRUE STORY OF HACKTIVISM

PETER BURNETT

 **EYEWEAR** PUBLISHING

First published in 2017
by Eyewear Publishing Ltd
Suite 333, 19-21 Crawford Street
London, W1H 1PJ
United Kingdom

Graphic design by Edwin Smet
Author image by Okashy
Printed in England by TJ International Ltd, Padstow, Cornwall

Eyewear wishes to thank Jonathan Wonham for his generous patronage of our press.

Set in Bembo 12 / 16 pt
ISBN 978-1-912477-01-2

WWW.EYEWEARPUBLISHING.COM

'World War III is a guerrilla information war with no division between military and civilian participation.'
Marshall McLuhan, 1970

'The question arose this morning, about the problem of whether the extension of the network, especially by electronics, might not abolish individual privacy.'
Alan Watts, 1970

'I don't want to live in a world where everything I say, everything I do, everyone I talk to, every expression of creativity and love or friendship is recorded.'
Edward Snowden, 2014

'We have done to ourselves fundamentally, what the terrorist wanted done but could never achieve. No other country in the world could have done to us what we have done to ourselves.'
William Binney, 2015

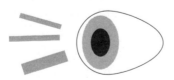

CONTENTS

INTRODUCTION

'Secrets are lies, sharing is caring,
and privacy is theft.'
The Circle, Dave Eggers (2013)

See what Dave Eggers has done there. He's taken that most perennially apt quote from George Orwell's *1984*[*]: 'War is peace. Freedom is slavery. Ignorance is strength.' And he's turned it to face our electronic social media. What he's saying is that our willingness to believe in a helpful government, and helpful social media corporations, will end us all. Neither state nor Internet is what it could be, nor what we believe it to be, and through double-speak, for either profit or control, our freedoms are being impaired. Correlate what you will from that, but I argue that with this level of control imposed upon us, we could be experiencing significantly more cyclopean political domination than we've ever experienced. The question remains: is someone (i.e. the usual suspects – state and corporations) doing this to us, or are we doing it to ourselves?

This book is about the individuals who have defied the government control and corporate commodification of the Internet. The war on privacy has been going on for longer than the War on Terror and the frontline is your phone, your computer, the world's data centres, and the airwaves and network cables themselves. As well

[*] The original title is *Nineteen Eighty-Four* but the author uses the more informal *1984* in this book interchangeably, as in the film version.

as direct assaults, in this war we see propaganda and the legal system playing an indirect role, and we'll be asking if the law should be above the law. On news websites, blogs and television shows the war on privacy never quite ends, so much so that you can follow it every day. Part of my message will be: 'ha ha ha, there is no privacy, and there never will be.'

A headline from January 2017 ran: 'Trump signs 'no privacy for non-Americans' order' (*The Register*, 26th January 2017).

This article referred to an executive order that specifically noted that privacy protections would not include those who are not US citizens or permanent residents in America. Every week there are new developments as technology races against the law and computing power and data services become more complex, more useful, and more dangerous. It's amazing what the Internet has become, but what sort of human beings will evolve as a result, and who do we have to blame for the clearly overwhelming effect it is having? To ask these questions is to enter a morass of contradictions, legal challenges, hopes and fears. Many people (or we may now call ourselves users, consumers or ambulatory data-sets) delight in the benefits of the new smart world and disdain idiotarian complaints which ferment opposition by arguing for:

- Respect for individual autonomy!
- Anonymous speech!
- The right to free association!

All of this and more must be balanced against reasonable concerns like law enforcement, but I have the impression that nobody hears, nobody cares, and the occupation of our dataspace continues.

The above story from *The Register* pointed to yet another new and largely ignored directive, which in this case contradicts the Privacy Shield, a framework used by Google and Dropbox among others, designed to facilitate the transfer of personal data between the EU and US by businesses.

In short, in trying to penetrate this new decision, I was reminded of how overwhelming the war on privacy is and how confusing the concept of privacy has become, because there are so many fronts and so little resistance. I would like to find out why this is and why the billions of smartphone users in the world accept the tech they are given with gladness and no dread. We don't know exactly what privacy is, even though we fear we've lost it. We concede privacy for services like Facebook and we're pleased to think that the widespread data capture carried out by our smartphones is catching terrorists.

Meanwhile, privacy is an intricate labyrinth of legal, philosophical and social debate entangled in acronyms and legal declarations, with the main players being writers, researchers, politicians, hackers and government spying agencies. We weren't warned that our privacy was going to suffer as a result of the Internet, but at the heart of this grave new world is a culture which seeks to find out everything about us.

Andrew Grove, the co-founder of the Intel Corporation put it wryly when he said: 'This wasn't the information that people were thinking of when they called this the information age.'

Privacy is nebulous, but received opinion is that it is what each of us sacrifices in order to catch the bad guys – isn't it? The other great intention already entrenched in our thinking is that our personal data leakage is some kind of trade-off. We all know this personal data is being siphoned up by everything from children's toys to parking meters, and yet we don't mind because there is nothing we can do and well, it may all be to our good. We also say that we are happy for our data to be collected, because of the free services we get in return, like Facebook, but I would think about that quite hard if I were you. Access to the Internet and its services is not comparable with data leakage. In using the Internet you are already paying your Internet service provider (ISP) a large fee for what may be a slow connection, accompanied by poor customer service. Many of you have no choice in ISP because some regions lack competition, but even in places where there is choice, all ISPs appropriate and process data in far greater quantities and higher detail than any other type of online company. Not only do ISPs capture data, but they capture metadata too, which is just as useful, as we shall see later. Do please consider these Internet service providers as we investigate this subject; the ISPs, more than any of the other tech giants, are getting good value here as they inspect, capture, and sell nearly every one of the millions of pieces of data we daily serve them. It is not, in my opinion, a fair trade off, and as I often find myself saying to friends who have fallen into wage slavery or a mean-assed love relationship: *you are worth so much more than that.*

Nobody likes to feel trapped, however, even when they are, so I imagine denial plays a part. After all, if you were to take these issues as seriously as you perhaps ought to, then you might wind up like hacker Buckminster Emptier, who writes of themself:

> I have eschewed all Google products (including search, which I abandoned about 2004), all Apple products, Microsoft products, smartphones, tablets, etc. I purchase everything in cash and have never owned an actual credit card. I won't patronize a bar or restaurant that uses CCTV. I don't socialize with people who have smartphones or similar devices, I cover my webcam, I've physically removed my microphone, and I don't do any professional work that would further the use of proprietary software or intrusive technologies.
> (*2600*, Volume 34, #2, Summer 2017)

When I first read this, I wondered if it was a joke; a person who through choice can visit only a small number of urban locations, associate with virtually no one in the Western world, and who can never work in any environment that uses Windows, Apple, etc.? For 99% of us this would be impossible, if not torturous. In fact, it sounds more iron-handed and astringent a life than could ever be produced by your average totalitarian nightmare. Who could live like this, isolated, probably ridiculed and almost certainly labelled as paranoid, even in the face of what can be demonstrated to be rational concerns?

But Buckminster Emptier's story is a real one, and they argue that they're living a happy and productive life without these things, doubtless as an example to the rest of us, who are surely en route to hell in one big-data handcart.

In practice, there aren't even any fixed definitions of privacy either, because privacy isn't real – it's only something that occurs when something else happens, like the Internet. Privacy takes in copyright and security, and it is probably key to your wellbeing. Just as your thoughts are private until you share them, so are your location, your friends, your conversations, your plans, your political beliefs, your sex life, your property and your story. Privacy is contained, we should have to imagine, in Terms of Service documents like Apple's iTunes TOS, which runs to about 20,000 words, roughly a third of the length of this book, and today more than anything, privacy means data.

It would be handy, therefore, to consider what our data really is while we test the validity of Buckminster Emptier's sober stance, as data is a more wide-ranging subject than the four letters of the word might suggest.[1]

1 The singular, *datum*, runs to five letters!

The first tier of data about ourselves that we may wish to consider as private might include our names, addresses, dates of birth, and the state-generated codes that identify us as unique, such as National Insurance numbers in the United Kingdom, passport numbers and Social Security information in the US. Most of these details are typically kept private, but I hope I will show we are now in a world in which this information is no longer private, or can be considered to be our information alone.

A second tier of data concerns our communications, which we may or may not have previously held as private. Ever since telephony we've all known that calls can potentially be recorded and swept for other data, however we have never expected this to be routine. As the volume of communication increases, and as communication and data markets grow, we are coming closer to a world in which your work routine, your family and your self could virtually be recreated by artificial intelligence, if we ever needed to leave this planet and start a new one.

A third tier of data concerns our habits. We didn't know until recently that everything we buy and everything we look at online, like details of where we go and who we meet, amounts to data that is not and may never be private. You may be resigned to the fact that all this data is collected, but there is bound to be some of it that will make you uncomfortable. Everybody, presumably, has something they would rather wasn't shared.

Finally, it might be worth considering our thoughts, which we may also wish to keep private. All the above data is at the present time being used by computer systems to make accurate statements and predictions about us. It is easy to see these artificial intelligence applications as marketing tools that meet needs and cut costs, but A.I. can do much more we haven't thought of yet. Creative writing isn't always an accurate predictor, but for over a century, science fiction novels have consistently told us that the loss of privacy may be one of the establishing factors of a possible despotic future.[2]

Putting it bluntly, then, if you accept that privacy is a thing of the past, and I am arguing that you must, all that remains unknown of you is the very real parts that remain private, these being your thoughts.

Our best bet here might be to understand privacy as over, leaving us to navigate what is left. This is the opinion of one in particular who has a massive vested interest in us relinquishing our inner thoughts, Mark Zuckerberg, who said in an infamous 2010 speech:

> People have really gotten comfortable not only sharing more information and different kinds, but more openly and with more people. That so-

---

2 To wit I cite: Yevgeny Zamyatin, *We* (1924); Aldous Huxley, *Brave New World* (1932); George Orwell, *Nineteen Eighty-Four* (1949); Philip K. Dick, *Eye in the Sky* (1957), John Brunner, *Stand on Zanzibar* (1968) and follow ups; *Ubik* (1969), Bob Shaw, *Other Days, Other Eyes* (1972); *A Scanner Darkly* (1977); Bruce Sterling, *Islands in the Net* (1988); David Brin, *Earth* (1990); Paul J. McAuley, Arthur C. Clarke, *The Light of Other Days* (2000); *Whole Wide World* (2001); Charles Stross, *Glasshouse* (2006); Cory Doctorow, *Little Brother* (2008), *Walkaway* (2017).

cial norm is just something that has evolved over time.

(*The Guardian*, 11th January 2010)

Deciding to reclaim privacy is not an easy option, but it will always be helpful to know who is watching, which is why this book talks about both the state and the data corporations, and does its best to describe what their interest might really be.

The other third parties after your data may be said to include malicious hackers, but these are small fry by the scope and standards of the first two, who, legally and with your consent, may have access to your every digital trace. I know hackers, and on the whole they are not malicious. If they are interested in our security it is only in order to improve it, even if we are encouraged to be scared of what we feel they know, and what they can do. Hackers, however, drive the progress of human civilisation and I'd like to introduce you to a few, certainly those who, like Buckminster, are working against the mighty tide of obscurity that is already here.

It's tricky to pin down, but the concept of online privacy is an abstraction that we can't feel or understand. Is complete security or privacy possible?

If we answer no, then what level of compromise is the most effective for the most parties, or will someone always be at an advantage? And if we answer yes, do we have to return to a previous age and live like poor Bucky, never going to town and stuck using niche encryption technologies and obscure open-source operating systems in order to conduct the most basic of online activities?

Finally, has a new inequality already emerged since most people are unable to afford the security used by corporations and governments, making even reasonable privacy out of reach?

> I think there's another motive for the surveillance: to protect power and wealth from the majority of Americans who have neither.
> (Joe Lauria, *Huffington Post,* April 2014)

If you look at your smartphone or computer as a hacking tool and as a terminal in a global network, you will begin to see what I mean. In the meantime, your computer and smartphone are seen by you as passive devices that are the subject of hacks, rather than what they are – devices equally capable of carrying out these operations.

This view can only encourage us to see the intelligent devices which are increasingly running the show as the portals through which we are viewed, as well as the windows to the world we want them to be; this book sheds light on this apparent contradiction, and argues that governments must do more to preserve privacy rights while endeavouring to protect their citizens, and offer them as much inclusion in terms of information.

> The first and last thing I do every day,
> is see what strangers are saying about me.
> (*Meatspace*, Nikesh Shukla, 2014)

I do hope you enjoy this book then. I have been inspired to write it first by the science fiction novels that I have enjoyed all of my life, but which in the words of Andrew O'Hagan, have now become fake, because they are almost nostalgic in the efforts they made to warn us. (*The Guardian* 17th June 2017).

I have also been inspired by all of the characters I describe within, all real people and with the tragic exception of Aaron Swartz, still among us — at time of writing. I am inspired by these people for their work, and because they have brought so much to our attention, often at great personal sacrifice. It is a sad world, really, that has arrived, because a certain type of discourse has now gone, and even the most relaxed among us are moved to suspicion when they begin to ask themselves about privacy. It is a sad world in which we are simultaneously focused on watching ourselves and others, almost policing ourselves it appears, and where we are all entertainers, politicians and, worst of all I find, perennially divided by social sharing and online debates.

'We are now at the point,' continues Andrew O' Hagan, 'where privacy might be the only corrective we have to the political forces embezzling our times.' (*The Guardian*, 17th June 2017).

CHAPTER 1 WORLD WAR WEB

Julian Assange, Jeremy Hammond
and #Anonymous Activism

> 'People should understand that WikiLeaks has
> proven to be arguably the most trustworthy new
> source that exists, because we publish primary
> source material and analysis based on that primary
> source material. Other organizations, with some
> exceptions, simply are not trustworthy.'
>
> Julian Assange

When we relate the notion of privacy to that of interests we stumble upon an immediate contradiction in the case of our governments. Most of us would agree that at some level, our governments should be open by default and only secret when it is necessary. The reasons for such government secrecy might include defence issues, criminal investigations, and occasional matters of diplomacy. In reality, however, our governments are run by people who have faults, operate faulty systems, and who often feel the need to obscure matters from the public for uncounted and multifarious reasons.

One historically consistent aspect of this disagreement is that if a government doesn't have its own offices of openness and departments responsible for the free access of information, then the public will create them. If the governments of the world don't like these open repositories of data, then there will inevitably exist a quarrel between those who seek to publish information in the public interest and the governments' own, often harsh, attempts to clamp down on what they thereafter class as their 'security'.

It is of course a mainstay of state power that what is illegal for the people should also be illegal for the government, and although we can conceive of exceptions, these exceptions should be notable only by their rarity.

I'm arguing that these exceptions should be rare because if you logically define all the areas in which governments have the legitimate right to privacy, everything else may be defined as 'our information'. This is to say that everything that is done outwith these several parameters in which we might allow our state leaders privacy, belongs to us – how much it costs – who carries it out – and what the processes are.

I know you are laughing now, because both the hardest conservatives and the softest liberals among us understand that the whole point of government is power, and that there is an easily grasped equation between secrecy and power, but this is where the citizenry can excel and even rise to fight.

Beginning in 2006, WikiLeaks made a powerful stab at increasing government transparency by releasing to the public documents that had in general been deliberately removed from sight – documents that showed the corrupted workings of Icelandic and Swiss banks, human rights violations in Kenya, and chemical dumping by oil company Trafigura in Africa. Other high profile documents from these same sources have included the *Standard Operating Procedures for Camp Delta* manual from the US Army, issued to soldiers dealing with prisoners at Camp Delta (2007); emails from staff at the University of East Anglia's Climate Research Unit which appeared to show that scientists engaged in various dodges and ploys to bolster arguments that global warming is real and man-made (2009); the 13,500 strong membership list of the far-right British National Party (2008); and Twin Towers pager data, which was released to much controversy in 2008.

WikiLeaks' success relies on the fact that its encrypted electronic dropbox accepts but does not solicit anonymous sources of information, and thus WikiLeaks encourages the activity of whistle-blowers, disaffected insiders, undercover journalists and other similarly motivated parties. Virtually none of WikiLeaks' activities are without controversy however, and already in my short list of greatest hits, you could ask, for example, how it is that the pager data of the victims of 9/11 could be said to be in the public interest, and under what circumstances the membership of a perfectly legal political party could and should be legitimately deprived of their privacy?

Although WikiLeaks is associated with one person, the Australian Internet activist Julian Assange, who founded it and who remains its editor-in-chief and director, the real significance of WikiLeaks is not in one person but in the fact that such an organisation would not have to exist at all in a society in which governments were free with the material they generated. Further, and in the cases of the corporations like Trafigura and other organisations such as the Church of Scientology, WikiLeaks acts as a resource for investigative journalists.

That WikiLeaks is, properly speaking, a journalistic organisation occasionally raises an eyebrow, because WikiLeaks does not publish material that we are used to seeing in journalistic format. According to WikiLeaks' own website, its goal is 'to bring important news and information to the public.' It goes on: 'One of our most important activities is to publish original source material alongside our news stories so readers and historians alike can see evidence of the truth.'

The functional aspect to this leaks website, which includes the electronic dropbox, endeavours to ensure than journalists and whistle-blowers are not jailed for revealing sensitive or classified documents. Since its inception, WikiLeaks has continued its business on this model and while people like myself tend to see it as a public service, our superiors, public execs and governments like to see it as a criminal organisation – a charge which rocketed to stratospheric levels in 2010 when the website released video footage shot from helicopter gunships in Iraq, in which the American military were shown shooting people who appeared to be civilians, including Reuters employees.

The Iraq War Document leaks shamed the US government because their openness was stunning; there was a Pentagon-peddled tale on one side and there was video evidence on the other. In between the truth and the lie stood the macabre military spokesman Mark Kimmitt and the awful chairman of the Joint Chiefs, Peter Pace, ring-fencing the story with lies.

> Find a man who'd been tortured and you'd be told it was terrorist propaganda; discover a house full of children killed by an American air strike and that, too, would be terrorist propaganda, or 'collateral damage', or a simple phrase: 'We have nothing on that.'
>
> (Robert Fisk, *Independent*, 23rd October 2010)

As if it weren't bad enough for the public to hear gunship pilots making jokes about dead civilians there were numerous further details that emerged when the helicopter videos became public. These included the fact that there had been an estimated 15,000 civilian deaths that had not been previously admitted by the US government (Iraq War Logs, 2nd January 2012) and the fact that the same US authorities had failed to investigate hundreds of reports of abuse, torture, rape and even murder by Iraqi police and soldiers (*The Guardian,* 23rd October 2010). One report released by WikiLeaks showed that the US military had cleared an Apache helicopter gunship to open fire on Iraqi insurgents who were trying to surrender

23

(Bureau of Investigative Journalism, 23rd October 2010), while a number of documents showed how US troops killed almost 700 civilians for coming too close to checkpoints, and these civilians included pregnant women and the mentally unwell (Al Jazeera English, 23rd October 2010). Interfaced with this was evidence of civilian deaths committed by contractors, such as Blackwater (*New York Times,* 23rd October 2010), and allegations of unrestricted torture and mistreatment of prisoners in the hands of the Iraqi police. Although Blackwater changed its name first to XE Services in 2009, and then to Academi in 2011, it was already known from the global publicity it generated in 2007 when a group of its employees killed 17 Iraqi civilians and injured 20 in Nisour Square, Baghdad, for which four contractors were convicted of voluntary manslaughter and first-degree murder.

Referring to my previous discussions on transparency and power, I feel we are obliged by these and other documents to ask once more, what exactly is being done in our names? I ask this because as the reputation of WikiLeaks increased, its trove of documents showed with no ambiguity that our governments were and are keeping far too many things secret.

There is a further and more intoxicating tension at work here, because this information has at times even led to popular revolutions. One of the US cables released by WikiLeaks, titled *Corruption in Tunisia: What's Yours is Mine* and dated 23rd June 2008, exposed the long-established venality of Tunisia's President's family, its reach into business and its penchant for transcending the rule of law, all of which led to that government's downfall and the subsequent protest that swept the Middle East.

To use a phrase popularised by the lower reaches of the Internet, the US government were colossally butt-hurt by WikiLeaks, and their immediate and ongoing reaction has been to go on the offensive. The common croon in defending mass surveillance is that a person will only make something secret if they have something to hide – but of course the same applies to our governments and the more they protested and called for the arrest and trial of Julian Assange, the more it became apparent that they had plenty they wished to hide.

The secrets that emerged from the WikiLeaks releases on the US government were on the whole banal, but within them there were confidences that would still shame even the most obdurate and pitiless of tyrants. These included details of torture practises – still very much denied by the US administration despite obvious evidence to the contrary – and other illegal acts, such as the practise of so-called 'double-clicking', a phrase which refers to the extermination of wounded soldiers on a battlefield, an action which is against the Geneva Convention.

For his role in highlighting such stratagems, it is not surprising how many US public officials have called for Julian Assange's own execution, and in the months following the release of the Iraq War Logs a long line of would-be media exterminators also stepped up to denounce Assange. This included radio host Glenn Beck, political commentator and old media type Bill O'Reilly, entertainer and radio host Rush Limbaugh, and Eric Bolling of *Fox News*, who called for Assange to be hanged in public.

Political and media anger has not just been restricted to these few greasy media grinders however, especially in the US – but what does the government and their co-opted media wish to prosecute Julian Assange for, exactly? Assange was certainly not the thief of the information he published and as a publisher he had First Amendment freedom to release what he did, as do the hundreds of other news organisations that have subsequently reported on and disclosed material from WikiLeaks. The logical consequence of any Assange inquisition would therefore be a virtual news shutdown that would have to take place if the publishing of this information was deemed to be illegal. Although the idea of blacking out the news is too madly exorbitant to be of practical use – and as such it would have to include the banning of this book – it now remains the only way our governments can ensure that their secrets remain classified and unseen.

I would further contend that all of this outrage and high-level dudgeon did not entirely emerge from the most famous of the WikiLeaks releases – instead, however, came to a head when it looked like a set of Bank of America leaks were imminent. Of course, the two most famous of WikiLeaks releases were arguably the helicopter gunship video associated with Chelsea Manning (known as the 'Collateral Murder' release) and the details of the US spying on the United Nations, which was known as the National Humint Collection Directive. This latter release from 2009 pointed to a confidential cable originating from the United States Department of State under US Secretary of State Hillary Clinton's name, which ordered US diplomats to spy on top UN officials. The intelligence information the diplomats were ordered to gather included biometric information such as DNA, fingerprints, and iris scans, passwords, and personal encryption keys, credit card numbers, frequent flyer account numbers, and work schedules, and targets included the foreign diplomats of US allies as well as the Secretary General of the UN.

However, these documents were not completely classified in the first instance, and referred to many things that people suspected anyway, and thus it is, I would argue, that although few remember the timing now, the fever pitched squealing began true and proper when Assange announced that a release concerning the Bank of America was imminent in late 2010 and early 2011. This is indeed when the bodily waste made physical contact with the electric-powered oscillating air current distribution device.

Despite the threat of a Bank of America cache being published by WikiLeaks, nothing materialised, and even though the Bank of America leak has been called by some a hoax (CNBC, 26th April 2011) I feel that the threat in itself was enough to reveal the enemy's hand.

Thus it was alleged in the summer of 2011 by Daniel Domscheit-Berg, a former colleague of Julian Assange, that the source-protection system used by WikiLeaks was not adequate, and at the time, the WikiLeaks Twitter account reported that Domscheit-Berg had destroyed material that he felt could not be safely released. This included, it is said, a copy of the entire US no-fly list, US intercept arrangements for over a hundred internet companies, and leaks from inside around 20 neo-Nazi organizations (Reuters, 22nd August 2011). This was a relief for the Bank of America and its affiliates, because whether the material existed or not, the bank's stock had already dropped 3% the previous November when it was reported that leaks were possible, indicating the strength of what is now called the new media. This was a moment of profound interest then, showing that when an organisation with such proven authority as WikiLeaks so much as threatened a certain release, a drop in market confidence and financial loss were the result.

In his 2011 book, *WikiLeaks and the Age of Transparency*, Micah Sifry argues that Internet technology will make governments and corporations open in spite of themselves, and he describes many projects such as opensecrets.org, maplight.org and govtrack.us — all of which monitor such activity, but all of which fail to work to any great effect because governments and their sponsors are fighting against them. We have all heard of WikiLeaks, but alongside it there is a substantial citizen movement that seeks to hold authority to account, and even though these organisations proliferate, their work is not well known.

In the UK we have mysociety.org, which champions open data, just as we have theyworkforyou.com, which tracks the activity of British members of Parliament, just as they-know.org holds information about state data mining and helps people with freedom of information requests.

These institutes, websites and organisations are premised on freedom of information, but the technology that powers them is nothing without the ongoing reform of the media and the eventual reform of government and corporate business practice. For many, the work of WikiLeaks and other disclosure websites is simply divisive; political hawks and those in power will condemn WikiLeaks not for what it publishes but for its methodology and its desire to call authority to account. Others, such as myself, will celebrate the fact that WikiLeaks exposes the hypocrisy, ambitions, and deceit of the world's corrupt empire builders.

Browsing the collected body of WikiLeaks releases, readers will see the different ways the US government keeps its power and will immediately notice a strong emphasis on the Middle East, notably in Iraq and Syria. We find that the UN reported in 2011 that in Iraq US forces had handcuffed Iraqi children, shot them in the head and then called in an airstrike to conceal the crime. We see a report on the Abu Ghraib prison that finds numerous incidents of criminal abuses of detainees. We read how the State Department's US-Middle East Partnership Initiative sponsored ongoing Syria-specific projects to undermine the Syrian government, and a 2006 cable from the US *chargé d'affaires* at the US embassy in Damascus to the Secretary of State and the President reveals the proposed US strategy for ousting the Syrian government, a plan which seems to show that the *chargé* is urging the US government to fan sectarian tensions between Sunni and Shia Muslims, even though he knew what this could lead to.

It appears then that without WikiLeaks, America and its allies such as Great Britain would be hiding behind thousands of dark secrets that have played unreasonably on other countries and large businesses alike, and anyone who cares to take the time to look at the WikiLeaks info will find a wealth of information and analysis that will make them think twice about the assumed bases for international relations.

WikiLeaks data is easy to locate online at wikileaks.org and it is now such a huge cache of material that it covers every aspect of global and national political affairs.

Know also that the website wikileaks.org is readily searchable, contains over 10 million documents and includes information on your own government and country, wherever you are, and it is not illegal for you to view it!

Of course, secrets are only as secure as the least trustworthy person that knows them, which in essence makes them not very secret at all. To pretend otherwise would be folly, and to compound this, governments do not simply have whistle-blowers, leakers and journalists to contend with, but a new breed of activist also.

The young Julian Assange perfectly embodied the spirit of this new type of activism when as a teenager in the 1980s he enjoyed testing the limits of what was possible with home computers, including the Commodore 64 which he reportedly used to explore the growing world of computer networks in an age when there were no websites at all.

It's worth defending the hacker ethos because without hackers we would have nothing at all in terms of technology. When I was growing up, being a hacker was a good thing – some hackers were our teachers and they encouraged the dismantling of technology in order to establish how things worked. Hackers have long advocated what is known as 'out of the box' thinking – innovative ways to use technology to achieve new and surprising ends, as well as solving problems. As the world's computer networks took shape in the 1990s and several hackers became well known for various feats of daring, the emphasis upon the term 'hacker' shifted from something good to something bad, as exampled in two 1999 speeches by Bill Clinton in which hackers were intentionally demonised for the first time.

It was during the Clinton presidency that the

world first became aware of the widespread possibilities of computers and connectivity, but perhaps an opportunity was lost when control and surveillance became the administration's preferred route. Yes, I would rather that hackers were at this point identified as our friends and closest advisors, but a demonisation began and as a result we were invited to trust the state, while the hacker was styled as the outsider, the outlier and ultimately the menace.

The Clinton presidency saw the introduction of three especially pertinent technological clampdowns:

1. **The Clipper Chip**: this was a set of electronic components that was developed by the United States National Security Agency (NSA) as an encryption device, with a built-in backdoor, intended to be adopted by telecommunications companies for voice transmission. The plan was that any new telephone or other device would be fitted with a Clipper Chip which would be given a cryptographic key, that would then be made available to the government. If government agencies established their authority to listen to a communication, then the key would be given to those agencies, who could then decrypt all data transmitted by that particular telephone. The Clipper Chip was announced in 1993 but by 1996 was entirely defunct partly

due to the work of the Electronic Privacy Information Center and the Electronic Frontier Foundation, and thereafter because it was rejected both by consumers and manufacturers.

2. **CALEA**: The Communications Assistance for Law Enforcement Act was a wiretapping law that was passed in 1994 which forced telecommunications carriers and manufacturers to modify and design their equipment, facilities, and services to ensure that they have built-in capabilities for targeted surveillance. In 2006, after two years of legal disputes, CALEA was reframed to include the United States government's ability to monitor VoIP and broadband Internet communications – which permits the monitoring of web traffic as well as phone calls.

3. **The Communications Decency Act**: The Communications Decency Act was the first act introduced in response to the rise of Internet pornography. As indecency in TV and radio broadcasting was already regulated by the Federal Communications Commission and the broadcasting of offensive speech was restricted to certain hours of the day, it was felt that something similar should be introduced to cover the Internet. The CDA, which affected both the Internet and cable television, marked the first attempt to

expand regulation to these new media, and basically used ancient tools to tackle futuristic issues. The actual freedom interest protected in this act was the fundamental right for consumers to choose whether they were exposed to obscene content or not, instead of having a tech enterprise make that choice for them, pretending that is freedom, when it was not.

The intent was clear in the 1990s then, that the Internet was going to be policed, and while this is understandable, comments made by Bill Clinton in 1999 on the subject of 'Keeping America secure for the 21st century' included the following statement, which was in my opinion the cornerstone set down to properly demonise hackers, and identify this previously non-criminal group as the potential villains of the information age:

> Last spring, we saw the enormous impact of a single failed electronic link, when a satellite malfunctioned – disabled pagers, ATMs, credit card systems and television networks all around the world. And we are already seeing the first wave of deliberate cyberattacks – hackers breaking into government and business computers, stealing and destroying information, raiding bank accounts, running up credit card charges, extorting money by threats to unleash computer viruses. (William J. Clinton, 22nd January 1999)

The idea that hackers were the enemy was never before this moment expressed, and yet since this time, the idea of the hacker as the enemy has prevailed in the public imagination. The speech, delivered before the National Academy of Sciences, classed hackers with other 'enemies of peace' including users of chemical and biological weapons, such as the attackers who used poisoned gas on the Tokyo subway in 1995.

It was in the 1990s also that the governments of the West started to accept that the next world war was going to be waged on the Internet – at least this is what President Clinton's advisers told him at the time, a fact which prompted the president to request $2.8 billion of a budget to go toward fighting 'exotic forms of terrorism', which included online attacks.

Hackers however, as I wish to remind you, are in general curious, sceptical, radical and generally seek positive change, as opposed to criminality.

As is the case with some other hackers, Assange began as a young person exploring places in the net he shouldn't have been and consequently got into trouble for doing so – but he quickly matured and turned these skills to focus on good. In 1987 Assange began hacking under the name Mendax and during this time he accessed the networks of the Pentagon and other US Department of Defence facilities, as well as those of companies like Citibank, Lockheed Martin, Motorola, Panasonic, and Xerox.

Being of a similar generation, I would like to argue that Assange grew up in an age when almost every-body who was interested in computers was a hacker by default. Those who are hovering around their half-century will know what I mean because to make the most of the first home and office computers in the 1970s and 1980s, we usually had to learn BASIC (which first appeared in 1964), or Fortran (which first appeared in 1957) in order to experiment. What this means is that anyone using a home or office computer in the 1980s would have had to know the first elements of simple programming languages and this was the case until the Graphic User Interfaces (GUIs) of the 1990s began to evolve into what we have today, in conjunction with the mouse pointer – but it wasn't always that way.

In September 1991 Julian Assange's phone line was tapped – bear in mind that he was using a modem – and his home was raided and he was eventually charged in 1994 with 31 counts of hacking and related crimes. In December 1996, Julian Assange pleaded guilty to 25 of these charges (the other six were dropped), and he was released on a good behaviour bond, avoiding a penalty because he had shown no malicious or mercenary intent and had generally been hacking for his own curiosity.

It was then that this young technologist began to move his attention away from network flaws to what he perceived as wrongdoings of governments, and in these motivations – a combination of hacking skills employed to expose wrongdoing, and a desire to uncover the hidden workings of both machines and organisations – we can see a decisive move away from network penetration to more settled concerns about the abuses of technology by those in power, and how hacking and other abilities can become a corrective.

In a 2007 blog post on IQ.org, Julian Assange wrote:

> The whole universe or the structure that per-ceives it is a worthy opponent, but try as I may I can not escape the sound of suffering. Perhaps as an old man I will take great comfort in potter-ing around in a lab and gently talking to students in the summer evening and will accept suffering with insouciance. But not now; men in their prime, if they have convictions are tasked to act on them.

Not every hacker acting on these convictions is con-cerned with the legality of their actions and for those, the term 'hacktivist' has been coined as a catchy blend of the words 'hacker' and 'activist'. The term was first used in 1994 and there continues to be significant disa-greement over whether hacktivists are a force for good or not. Some definitions of hacktivism include acts of illegal access to private networks and forays into cyberterror-ism, while others say that hacktivism can simply refer to the use of technological hacking to affect social change.

Either way, the term 'hacktivist' refers to activists from across the political spectrum who have taken their fight to the Internet. Different people hack for different reasons and while some attack websites ('black hats') and others protect them ('white hats') there are always going to be a percentage of the population who want to explore technology for themselves, and do so from the inside.

There are plentiful ways by which information on wrongdoing can be brought to public attention, and it doesn't just happen by whistle-blowing. A whistle-blower must work from inside an organisation, whereas a hacktivist may well be trying to break into that organisation to obtain information they believe to be in the public interest. For those interested in exposing perceived and actual wrongdoing within states, corporations and other public and private bodies, the main point of contact across the world has for some time been the Anonymous movement, the rise of which is documented in the movie *We Are Legion* (Brian Knappenberger, 2012).

Anonymous originated around 2003 on the website 4chan and grew around the notion of a community of users simultaneously existing as a digitised global entity, taking part in pranks and activism. There was a time when Anonymous members – you can call them Anons – could be distinguished in public by the wearing of the stylised Guy Fawkes mask as exampled in the movie *V For Vendetta* (James McTeigue, 2006) – but these days the masks are fairly ubiquitous and stand for the basic values of public anonymity, or simply as a statement of rebellion. Anons probably know that there is no such thing as real anonymity, and that to believe in it would be a false sense of security, but for them it is all about the idea[3]. For those wishing to 'join Anonymous' the process is truly simple – merely obtain a Twitter or other social media account, place as your avatar any one of any number of variations of images of the Guy Fawkes mask, and start interacting with other Anons and participating in their campaigns, and you will be safely there.

There is plentiful information on #Anonymous and most of it is up for grabs in terms of reliability. There are at the same time, many standards, as well described I feel in this passage:

> Anonymous, inherently, is non-hierarchical. Rather than following a person, they follow an idea. The idea becomes the top level of the hierarchy and the people involved become the bottom level. When an idea comes along that they like, people will join together and act on it.
>
> Because we have a culture where there are good guys and bad guys, we demand that those labels be used, and that people be lumped into either one or the other, preferably those who agree with us and those who don't. The problem is that when we do that without understanding why it doesn't actually work that way, we unfairly prosecute people who were doing the 'right' thing, and wind up having to deal with people who have been mislabelled.

---

3 'You cannot arrest an idea.' @atopiary, Twitter (21.07.2011)

(aestetix, *2600*, Winter 2012)

What is truly positive about Anonymous is contained within the name. In an age when every person's moves and thoughts are tracked, there is much to be said for a place or a group where the importance of anonymity is paramount. Indeed, both privacy and anonymity have been sufficiently eroded since the 1980s when public surveillance took off, so much so that much of what Anons stand for is very obviously in the public interest. Although there is no credo, central leadership, or guide to Anonymous, their significance is huge insofar as it can attract individuals who in general oppose Internet censorship and control.

Quinn Norton in an article *Anonymous 101: Introduction to the Lulz* wrote in November 2011:

> I will confess up front that I love Anonymous, but not because I think they're the heroes. Like Alan Moore's character V who inspired Anonymous to adopt the Guy Fawkes mask as an icon and fashion item, you're never quite sure if Anonymous is the hero or antihero. The trickster is attracted to change and the need for change, and that's where Anonymous goes.

Often, we hear of Anons when they are arrested, and dozens have been charged with cyberattacks, most particularly in the US, UK, Australia, the Netherlands, Spain, and Turkey. The July 2011 arrest of the young

British hacker Jake Davis, known as Topiary, became a special rallying event and because of his popularity, not just within the Anonymous movement but with a public who were still coming to terms with the Internet, there sprang into being a fairly extensive #FreeTopiary movement and more importantly, a public debate about the necessity of policing the web.

One of the elder members of the movement is Chris Doyon (alias Commander X), who was arrested in September 2011 for a cyberattack on the website of Santa Cruz County, California, which had taken into custody several people who had occupied the Santa Cruz County courthouse after the city enacted a law restricting camping within the city limits. This law, of course, as Commander X pointed out, was not an attempt to hamper campers, but in fact criminalised public sleeping, and was thus an attack on the homeless community – and it is in fact a law that still stands. In 2017, X published the book *Behind The Mask: An Inside Look At Anonymous*, describing his life as a hacker on the run, in which he talks of many exploits including a daring attack against the government of Egypt during the Arab Spring of 2011, which he conducted from a San Francisco coffee shop:

> I programmed a 'spider' to crawl servers and harvest specific data. Mine was programmed to collect the fax numbers and E-Mail addresses of every single Egyptian. My spider, which I nicknamed 'Hazel' – was not only capable of doing

the task – but she could then separate the civilian from the government data. This would eventually allow Anonymous to wage psychological warfare on the Egyptian government while at the same time sending valuable information and encouragement to the Egyptian people…This led to a somewhat comical scene of me having to spend the night sleeping in an alley behind the coffee house so I could stay connected and keep Hazel running.

Like Anonymous, Commander X remains a divisive character but the idea of coordinating globally influential hacks while sleeping rough is enthralling, and his story encapsulates what is most exciting and most challenging about this activist movement which still persists.

Although Commander X continues to be on the run from the US authorities, others have been captured and imprisoned. Foremost among these is Jeremy Hammond, who was jailed for ten years in November 2013, for the theft of information from a private security company called Stratfor.

Stratfor, also known as Strategic Forecasting Inc, is an intelligence firm that collects and analyses data for government and corporate clients, who pay for access to their consultancy services. It's one of an informal and debatable legion of consulting firms that operate in a place where barriers between corporate and government responsibility are beclouded and made hazy. Whether or not they are a force for good or a repository of uber-concentrated foulness, the standard of Stratfor's research has been the subject of criticism, and where the company's findings have been reported in the media they have not always proven to be accurate.

But even where Stratfor's claims have been corroborated, information about how the company operates and whom it works with and for is still significant. When multinational corporations pay a private intelligence firm to spy on activists, that is newsworthy regardless of whether the company in question is able to accomplish those tasks. Similarly, what sources in governments and corporations around the world are happy to tell Stratfor in confidence is valuable regardless of its accuracy.

As an object example of this sort of intelligence collection by private agencies, ahead of the 2010 Winter Olympics in Vancouver, Coca-Cola asked Stratfor for information on PETA (People for the Ethical Treatment of Animals) activists and requested data on the likelihood that they would protest at the games. In the email requesting the intelligence, Coke's representative first thanked Stratfor for 'help with respect to the Korean Peninsula situation,' before listing several questions, including: 'To what extent will US-based PETA supporters travel to Canada to support activism?'

A separate group of emails show Stratfor offering advice to oil and gas companies who are dealing with environmental protests, including a presentation for energy giant Suncor on how to tackle opposition to exploitation of Canadian tar sands, a similar service to which had previously been pitched to Chevron. The emails show that corporations also use Stratfor – and presumably companies like them – to investigate competitors and individual employees.

As with other WikiLeaks publications, the Stratfor documents carry a theme of repressing democratic resistance, particularly in Western societies, and this is why it is important we know that Facebook, our email and so forth are potentially being watched. We have already seen this sort of spying and infiltration against the left in both America and the UK (Occupy, Animal Rights Groups) and the right (Tea Party, British National Party). Whereas terrorists don't tend to use Facebook, these dissenting groups do, and although they may do so with an expectation of minimal privacy, they should not expect their data to be used against them and their causes.

Stratfor and companies like it are therefore significant, because their activities define new battle lines. Firstly, Stratfor are a geopolitical intelligence and consulting firm who have had both corporate and government clients. What is of interest to journalists and activists here is the nature of these security contracts and what the companies are permitted to get away with simply because they are government contractors. There is a demonstrable need for journalists and publishers to be able to see and understand these revelations, so it is incumbent upon hackers and whistle-blowers to provide them data which will often be at the very least leaked without the company's consent – or sometimes as in the case of Stratfor, simply stolen.

Even the most cursory examination of this set up, in which private companies are paid by state agencies to carry out covert operations, begs examination.

To this end the Stratfor emails published by WikiLeaks in 2012-2013 are of such significance that they have their own special name – the Global Intelligence Files – or simply the GI Files. These documents are still online and in the hands of WikiLeaks, where journalists and citizens are at liberty to examine them and make their own minds up. Further, citizens can look at these materials without breaking the law, although as we will see in a later chapter one journalist at least has been arrested, charged and imprisoned for sharing a link to them.

The material within the stolen GI Files obtained from Stratfor by Jeremy Hammond contains secret information about the US government's attacks against Julian Assange and Stratfor's own attempts to subvert WikiLeaks, with more than 4,000 emails mentioning this subject alone. The Stratfor emails also expose links between private intelligence companies in the United States and government and diplomatic sources that appear to be offering Stratfor advance knowledge of global political events in exchange for money. Also from within the GI Files, as currently hosted by WikiLeaks, we can see how Stratfor recruited a world-wide network of informants who appear to have been paid via Swiss banks accounts and pre-paid credit cards – a list of covert and overt informants that includes government employees, embassy staff and journalists.

Most keenly of all, the Stratfor files show how a private intelligence agency works and how they target individuals for their corporate and government clients.

The example that WikiLeaks likes to mention is that of Stratfor monitoring the activities of Bhopal activists on behalf of the US chemical giant Dow Chemical – but other material of interest in this cache shows much more:

> • Some emails leaked from the GI Files hack show that Stratfor had been partnering with a former Goldman Sachs director, along with other informants, in order to benefit from what could be considered insider trading.
> • An email involving a Stratfor analyst stated that it had been established that officials in Pakistan's Inter-Services Intelligence agency knew of Osama bin Laden's safe house.
> • Emails from Stratfor's Vice-President for Counterterrorism and Corporate Security (and former Deputy Chief of the Department of State) Fred Burton, showed a secret US government indictment against WikiLeaks founder Julian Assange, while other emails cast doubt on the rape allegations against Assange.

These are a taste of the jaw-dropping material revealed in the Stratfor hack, and this collected body of alleged immorality obviously raises questions not only about the role of private security companies but the necessity of such intervention as activists such as Jeremy Hammond have made.

Born in 1985, Jeremy Hammond was attracted to computers early in life, and when he was a school pupil, opposition to the Iraq War motivated him to organise a school walkout and encourage about 200 students to leave class and take a train to join larger anti-war protests. After graduating, Jeremy Hammond founded hackthissite.org, which trains beginners in the very basic application of computer security measures. The site is so good, in fact, that a person with absolutely no knowledge of computing can visit it and learn some practical and basic skills in no time at all. What hackthissite.org provides is fundamental instruction in how websites and web protocols work. It's a little like owning a car, and being willing on occasion to look at its engine, either to fix or explore it.

Jeremy Hammond's first spell in prison occurred when he was 20 years old, after he had broken into a conservative website called Protest Warrior and stolen credit card numbers, intending to use them to charge donations to liberal and radical groups. Protest Warrior, which was primarily known for managing counter-protests in favour of the Iraq war, used legal approaches in spreading its message, but to counter them, Hammond illegally accessed the organisation's servers to obtain private information.

Hammond's activity continued in December 2010 when Visa, PayPal and MasterCard blocked payments and donations made to WikiLeaks, after Julian Assange published certain US State Department cables. Although these financial organisations had bowed to state pressure in refusing to process WikiLeaks donations, their actions upset many hacktivists and others connected with the Anonymous movement. Activists thereafter launched a series of distributed denial of service (DDoS) attacks against these banking corporations, using widely available website testing software to swamp the servers of the financial institutions, and effectively killing their websites for short periods. Fourteen defendants – known as the PayPal 14 – were later arrested and charged under the Computer Fraud and Abuse Act for their part in these attacks.

When it came to targeting Jeremy Hammond it was alleged that from December 2011 to March 2012, Hammond and his co-conspirators mounted a cyber assault on the website and computer systems of Stratfor. It's said that Hammond and these same co-conspirators stole confidential information, which included approximately 60,000 credit card numbers and associated data belonging to clients of Stratfor, who had signed up to their paid mailing list. Also included in this cache were Stratfor clients' user IDs and passwords, as well as emails belonging to Stratfor employees, and internal Stratfor corporate documents, which, as we have seen, contained in some instances evidence of potentially illegal activity. Thereafter it was alleged that Hammond used some of the stolen credit card data to make at least $700,000 worth of unauthorised charges and that he had publicly disclosed much of the data. After pleading guilty to one count of violating the Computer Fraud and Abuse Act, Hammond was sentenced in November 2013 to the maximum of ten years in prison, followed by three years of supervised release – although in his sentencing statement, Hammond said he was totally unaware of the Stratfor website's vulnerabilities until he was given them by another hacker, who was at that point under the supervision of the FBI.

This last intervention was a surprise to the hacker and activist community – but in a manner as typically dramatic as any moviemaker might imagine, Hammond had been in part set up, and information concerning the vulnerabilities of the Stratfor website had been passed to him by the FBI, via one of their narks, an informant named Hector Xavier Monsegur, also known as Sabu, who had been engaging in what with hindsight, looks like entrapment. Although the precise details are still sealed, the case against Jeremy Hammond and others associated with Anonymous relied heavily on the cooperation of the arch-stoolie Sabu, who worked for nine months in complicity with the FBI, and who instigated some of the attacks that Hammond and others would later be charged with.

Hector Monsegur himself was a talented computer hacker up until he was arrested on 7th June, 2011, and it was on the following day that he agreed to become an informant for the FBI and to continue his Sabu persona online in order to help the government build cases against any and all Anons it could catch. Not only did the FBI provide its own servers for the hacking to take place, but a court filing made by prosecutors in May 2014 claimed that Monsegur had prevented 300 cyberattacks, including planned strikes on NASA, the US military and media companies.

In his sentencing statement in November 2013, Jeremy Hammond acknowledged Sabu's involvement in his own case, saying:

> I had never even heard of Stratfor until Sabu brought it to my attention. Sabu was encouraging people to invade systems, and helping to strategise and facilitate attacks. He even provided me with vulnerabilities of targets passed on by other hackers so it came as a great surprise when I learned that Sabu had been working with the FBI the entire time.

The list of attacks instigated and coordinated by Hector 'Sabu' Monsegur while he was handled by the FBI is still sealed by court order but appears to have included the websites of several foreign governments. Hammond also stated:

> What the United States could not accomplish legally, it used Sabu, and by extension, me and my co-defendants, to accomplish illegally. The questions that should be asked today go way beyond what an appropriate sentence for Sabu might be: Why was the United States using us to infiltrate the private networks of foreign governments? What are they doing with the information we stole? And will anyone in our government ever be held accountable for these crimes?

As an Internet search will show you if you dare to type his name into your computer, Hector Monsegur is not so popular among Anons these days. This will surely be because while continuing to masquerade as a hacktivist after his arrest, Monsegur led the authorities to arrest several others associated with the hacker collective Anonymous, including Jeremy Hammond and two UK hackers, James Jeffery and Ryan Cleary.

What prosecutors called Monsegur's 'truly extraordinary' cooperation with the FBI included encouraging followers of his Twitter feed to take part in criminal activity, as well as betraying former comrades while instigating many of the attacks they would later be charged with.

Not everybody thinks that Internet security and freedom of information should be such an ongoing battle, and many would like to see co-operative methods employed in negotiating a world that would satisfy the requirements of both privacy activists and governments.

As it stands the situation is quite intractable however – hacktivists will continue to use every method at their disposal to reveal wrongdoing where they can, and governments and their contractors will continue to apply secrecy at will and pursue transparency only when it suits them or when they are forced to do so. Because of the Stratfor hack, some of the dangers of an unregulated private intelligence industry are now known. It has also been shown through WikiLeaks that Stratfor, for one, maintained a worldwide network of informants that engaged in invasive and perhaps illegal surveillance activities on behalf of multinational corporations.

For Internet activists and governments, the war on privacy is very much alive and unlikely to ever conclude. States will always fight transparency and claim rights to privacy which they will not permit citizens, and with the collusion of journalists, hackers will always sniff out corruption and seek to reveal it where they can.

The infamous 'Great Firewall of China' is a choice specimen of such governmental control. The GFW, which is a combination of legislative and technological actions taken to regulate the Internet in the country of China, is the main instrument used by the Chinese government to achieve Internet censorship. If a Chinese citizen searches for information on certain subjects, which might include Tibetan independence for example, her search might not only be blocked, but she could even be subject to a visit from the police. Other regulations include criminalising certain online speech and activities, blocking viewing of selected websites, filtering key words out of searches initiated from computers located in Mainland China, and requiring international online service providers to store their Chinese customer information within China.

All of this amounts to an invasion of privacy, and while many will simply accept it, others will remain outraged by it. Of those that will be outraged, there will also be a percentage who will begin to wonder how to circumvent it or seek to bypass it or overturn it somehow, and criminal or not, these are the individuals that best embody the hacker spirit that is so valuable to progress and liberty. It might not be you or me, because we may have neither the expertise nor the guts, but it is usually these individuals we have to thank for tipping the balance of power back in our own favour as Internet users. We wonder, however, when it comes to data collection and snooping, if a private citizen was using spying devices, or accessing Internet or cellphone traffic, would it be illegal?

If so, then it should also be illegal for security services and the police to use it without a specific warrant and in a controlled manner, such as specialist officers with some variety of neutral oversight present. Surely it is the case that the law cannot be above the law?

The final word in this chapter is offered to Jeremy Hammond:

> I realize that I released the personal information of innocent people who had nothing to do with the operations of the institutions I targeted. I apologize for the release of data that was harmful to individuals and irrelevant to my goals. I believe in the individual right to privacy – from government surveillance, and from actors like myself, and I appreciate the irony of my own involvement in the trampling of these rights.

CHAPTER 2 THE SURVEILLANCE STATE OF EMERGENCY

Blowing the Whistle: A brief history of state surveillance.

> The nature of the surveillance state is such that anything is suspicious – by definition you are always looking for suspicious activity – and so in the pathology of surveillance, you are always looking for more information.
>
> Thomas Drake

Did I laugh out loud earlier and joke that Internet privacy was a myth? At the very least, it may as well stand along those other husky and infamous oxymorons of our time such as Microsoft Works[4]; United Nations; personal computer; random order; Linux Complete; same difference; plastic glasses; Peace Force and my personal favourite: 'This page has been intentionally left blank'.

James Otis, Jr. (1725-1783) was a lawyer in colonial Massachusetts and an advocate of the patriotic American opinions that led to the American Revolution. Otis is more increasingly brought to bear on the discussion

---

4 Excuse the wilful misrepresentation but this is a popular joke among hackers, anons etc. Perhaps it is not even funny, as Microsoft's popularity relies on the fact that its contrivances work all too well. MS Works, which was built and sold as a low-cost office suite, was discontinued after 2007 after becoming increasingly untenable as Google began attracting users with its free Docs Web applications.

of privacy these days, as we try and master some of the foundational concepts pertinent to this idea, because in some senses, his work brought about some of the earliest legal declarations concerning citizens and their rights to privacy.

Otis wrote several pamphlets in the early phase of the Revolution and helped galvanize radical opposition to the British Empire. In *The Rights of the British Colonies Asserted and Proved* (1764) Otis went from an objection to a specific tax on sugar to an all-purpose argument in favour of natural rights and the consent of the governed. The Otis catchphrase 'taxation without representation is tyranny' became the basic patriot position and it's still a phrase we hear today; part of it is even printed on the standard-issue District of Columbia license plate. The argument is that nobody should pay tax and then fail to have a say in a government's activity.

Otis, who considered himself a loyal British subject, was outraged in the 1760s when the British government enacted new laws that were supposedly put in place to tackle smuggling. These laws introduced what were called Writs of Assistance, and these documents remain among the most intrusive search warrants that have ever been declared and amounted to permanent and transferable permits which allowed any British solider to search any American home, with neither warning nor due reason.

American colonists protested that these writs violated their rights as British subjects because not only could any property be searched at the whim of the holder, but those who carried out the searches were not responsible for any damage they caused. This put anyone who had such a writ above the law and with the writs being transferable, these powers were almost unlimited.

In his legal case against the Writs of Assistance, James Otis argued that in order for a search warrant to be issued, one must go to a judge, present some evidence and/or a probable cause and declare to that judge the reasons for the search. Such was the basic notion of privacy in 1770 – that people's homes, just as their own persons, were maintained at a reach from the state.

Although Otis lost his case, it was a highly influential episode which soon found official legal expression in the 1780 Massachusetts Declaration of Rights, which in turn formed the basis for the Fourth Amendment of the US Constitution – the one that includes the important provision: 'The right of the people to be secure in their persons, houses, papers, and effects, against unreasonable searches and seizures, shall not be violated'.

This statement in the Fourth Amendment is more sophisticated than it sounds as it overturned millennia of feudal, imperial and dictatorial powers by stating that governments could not act as they had done since before the reach of memory, and treat their citizens as objects with which they could do as they pleased.

While there isn't a specific British equivalent to the Fourth Amendment, most of these same protections do exist in UK law. In practical terms, the Fourth

Amendment and laws similar to it protect people from unreasonable searches and seizures by the government, and although it is not a guarantee of security it draws a line between the state and the individual and establishes the notion of privacy, the very idea that we are now seeing eradicated.

These new eighteenth century rights were a philosophically stimulating addition to our societies and offered brand new freedoms based on the secular philosophies of the day. What was established in the Fourth Amendment and similar expressions was the idea of privacy and most specifically a privacy specific to places and individuals.

Although intelligence has always been collected by governments, just as it has been collected by criminals, businesses and even private citizens, it is the governments who have been granted the responsibility of public safety. With this in mind, the tension between the public and private has escalated. Surveillance and its effects – as beautifully exemplified in the home telescreens in George Orwell's *1984*, which operated as both televisions and security cameras – has brought a conspicuous need for balance, most of which takes place through the law courts. On one side of the scales lie the possibilities of new technology and the capacity for information upon which states thrive, and on the other side is this relatively recent notion that there is such a thing as privacy at all.

It wasn't until the 1920s that the precursors of the modern national intelligence services were formed and from the start these services monitored local and international communication. In doing this, these budding spy agencies collected transmissions that existed largely outside of the home, even insofar as calls and messages travelled down some cables. The difference today is that because Internet and mobile technology have outgrown our wildest technological dreams, the security versus privacy debate no longer begins and ends at one's front door, as it did in the 1700s.

The first instance of a hi-tech governmental spy agency was the USA's Cipher Bureau – also known as the Black Chamber. The Cipher Bureau was established in 1919 and was set up to monitor international telegraphic communications, looking in particular for those which suggested a threat to the national security of the United States. Those familiar with the workings of the NSA as revealed by Edward Snowden will not be surprised to know that when the Chamber approached the largest communication company of its day asking if it could have complete access to every message handled by it, the company, the Western Union (as with Verizon and others today) was happy to comply.

In World War II when project SHAMROCK gave the Armed Forces Security Agency (which later became the NSA) full access to communications handled by Western Union, ITT and RCA Global, greater momentum was afforded the world of espionage, and several programs were introduced as temporary wartime measures. The SHAMROCK program, which collected all communications data entering and leaving the US, remained active until 1975, a full thirty years after its emergency powers should have expired. What this meant was that during these decades, millions of messages were intercepted and recorded with no search warrants being issued, and with no court oversight at all.

1975 is important, because the actions of Richard Nixon in in the years just previous had caused much of this to be reconsidered when it was discovered that he and his immediate predecessors in office had been using these resources to spy on political opponents, including Dr Martin Luther King Jr, feminist organisations, anti-colonial movements, and other left-leaners.

Thus it was that the Foreign Intelligence Surveillance Act (FISA) was passed in 1978, and a secret court was created which allowed warrants to be issued for surveillance of foreign nationals within the United States. In the implementation of this secret court, to which no voters, journalists or even governmental officers have access, Americans and others around the world are to thereby understand that government spying is going to happen regardless. This of course presents our governments as operating above the law, a fact that debases our now centuries-old concept of what a liberal, democratic state should be.

Does that mean that as social beings we are happy to live as a part of a lie? Do we live in a democracy that we know is unconstitutional, believing in a privacy that does not exist? Of course there is nothing quite like a secret court when it comes to the sound administration of justice! But within this framework, the Foreign Intelligence Surveillance Act of 1978 (FISA) has since been used to permit electronic surveillance and collection of 'foreign intelligence information' between 'foreign powers' and 'agents of foreign powers', which may still include American citizens and permanent residents suspected of crimes or people linked to those who are.

When applying for the authority for surveillance from the FISA court the government must show probable cause that the 'target of the surveillance is a foreign power or agent of a foreign power' if it wants to access people's communications. There have been questions, however, regarding the issuing of warrants by FISA and between 1975 and 2014, the secret court received over 35,500 requests for surveillance and denied a total of twelve of these. You can make of this ratio what you will, but it is difficult not to see the FISA court as a rubber-stamping green-light mechanism for domestic spying, as well as a detour around a constitution that is supposed to apply to citizens as much as it does their rulers.

At the same time as the FISA court was coming into being, a project called ECHELON was also commenced. ECHELON was originally the codename for an intelligence gathering and analysis network that the NSA and its partners in Britain, Canada, Australia and New Zealand operated through a system of automated interception posts across the planet. These countries – the so called Five Eyes – often abbreviated to FVEY – have led the way in global intelligence gathering since the 1970s, with the NSA and the GCHQ being the chief two partners. One of the benefits of the Five Eyes group is that as a point of principle (and law) governments are not supposed to spy on their own citizens. However, this special coalition of English-speaking spy agencies has meant that any partner in this group can ask another partner to spy on its citizens, allowing all five members to truthfully say that they do not spy on their own people.[5]

What we have here then, to continue this oxymoronic inheritance, are a set of shadow government agencies that purport to protect our freedoms and way of life by destroying our freedoms and way of life. And maybe that would be acceptable, if everybody within the democracy conceded to it.

Critically, however, ECHELON was operated without any official acknowledgement whatsoever. This meant that ECHELON began as a totalistic entity, with no legal oversight or legislative debate behind it, and carried out elite espionage with little oversight. Although ECHELON and its listening stations and other programs were a fundamental aspect of Cold War activity, the project did not end with the Cold War – and in fact its budget was increased in the later 1980s and 1990s. Public confirmation of much of this only became public as recently as 2015 when it was confirmed that ECHELON was part

5 The Five Eyes alliance also cooperates with groups of third party countries to share intelligence (forming the Nine Eyes and Fourteen Eyes), however Five Eyes and third-party countries can and do spy on each other. The other countries are as follows: For Nine Eyes add: Denmark, France, Netherlands and Norway. For Fourteen Eyes add: Belgium, Germany, Italy, Spain and Sweden.

of an umbrella program codenamed FROSTING, which was established by the NSA in 1966 to collect and process data from Soviet communications satellites, as well as from commercial satellites.

The secrecy of ECHELON was always well protected, despite there being a series of breaches in its security over the years, and despite it being operated for so long, it was still incumbent upon Edward Snowden to inform us what it was really doing, as late as 2015. Concerns about ECHELON have been voiced for decades, however. There is evidence that Canadian security services, for example, spied on at least two British cabinet ministers in 1983 on behalf of Prime Minister Margaret Thatcher; that the calls of Princess Diana were intercepted until she died; and that the conversations of Kofi Annan and Ban Ki-moon were among others which were routinely intercepted.

What is less known about ECHELON is that it is not entirely configured to spy on citizens in an effort to locate criminal or terrorist activities, because it has become known that ECHELON has been used for industrial espionage as well.

In 1998, a German company called Enercon developed (what it thought was) a secret invention which would allow people to generate wind-powered energy at a far cheaper rate than had been previously imagined. When Enercon tried to market its invention in the United States, it encountered a North American rival called Kenetech, which told them it had already patented a near-identical development, and this company served Enercon with a lawsuit forbidding them to market their development in the States. A public disclosure from an NSA employee, who appeared in silhouette on German television, subsequently revealed that the NSA had tapped the private link between Enercon's laboratory and their factory, and that NSA agents had supervised these plans being handed over to Kenetech.

At the same time, in September 1999, it was also revealed that by a similar special agreement, Microsoft (the butt of earlier and hugely unfair jokes by myself and other hackers) had inserted special keys into the Windows operating system. It appears that this had been going on from Windows 95 onwards and one must assume that it is still the case. In 1999 though, this was brought into the open thanks to the work of a computer scientist Andrew Fernandez, who had disassembled sections of the Windows instruction code and found two debugging symbols that had been left after testing. One of these debugging symbols was called KEY, while the other, the smoking gun, was called NSAKEY.

Whistle-blowing concerning the practises of our spy agencies is as old as the agencies themselves. In his book *War Is a Racket* (1935), Smedley Butler (1881-1940) described diverse US military operations that he argued were not about protecting democracy but about furthering the business interests of US banks and corporations. Butler compared these military activities to Al Capone-style mob hits on behalf of American corporations and their respective business interests, and although he continued his case against war profiteering, Butler was denounced in the press as a joker and a fantasist.

Similarly, in the UK in 1985, MI5 employee Cathy Massiter revealed that her supervisors at Century House in London had over-keenly interpreted which groups qualified as 'subversive', thus justifying surveillance against trade unions, civil liberty organisations and the Campaign for Nuclear Disarmament. Cathy Massiter also exposed the surveillance of Harriet Harman and Patricia Hewitt (while they were members of the National Council for Civil Liberties) and she paved the way for other British whistle-blowers, proving that 50 years after World War II, our spy agencies had settled on browbeating domestic peace activists and other internal political opponents.

The next significant British whistle-blower of this era was Annie Machon, a classics graduate from Cambridge University who was recruited by MI5 in 1991 and posted to their counter-subversion department. Annie Machon spent two years investigating militant Irish republicanism, before being reposted to the international counter-terrorist division, and in 1996 she and her colleague David Shayler resigned to blow the whistle on a series of alleged crimes committed by the agency spies, none of which were subsequently followed up by the Crown Prosecution Service. The material released by Machon and Shayler included secret MI5 files held on the government ministers, details of illegal MI5 phone taps, details of lying to the government by MI5, information on IRA bombs that could have been prevented, and details of an attempted Secret Intelligence Service assassination of Colonel Gaddafi of Libya.

In the US there has been a similar spritz of whistle-blowers over these decades, prominent among them being Thomas Drake, who was a senior executive at the NSA in the late 1990s and early 2000s when new tools were being developed to collect intelligence from the increasing flood of information then travelling out of the new digital networks.

Key to Thomas Drake's story is that he tried to play by the rules. Hoping in fact *not* to become a whistle-blower, Thomas Drake tried to do things in the right way by going through the agency's command chain to address his issues. In a way, Thomas Drake's example showed Edward Snowden what not to do as Drake first spoke to his bosses and attempted to deal with the issues he wished to raise through the Agency's own channels.

To put it briefly, Drake's issue within the NSA concerned two projects that were designed to intercept largely public communications – the TRAILBLAZER project and the THINTHREAD project. Within the Agency, Drake argued that he favoured the THINTHREAD project because it carried with it a theoretical ability to protect the privacy of US individuals while gathering intelligence. On the other hand, TRAILBLAZER – the program that was finally chosen – cost billions of dollars and crudely collected everything it could, with the contracting work to build it going to NSA-friendly contractors such as IBM, SAIC and Boeing.

Realising that he was uncomfortable with what he knew, Drake began to work through the legal processes that are prescribed for government employees who believe that questionable activities are taking place in their department, and in accordance with laws such as the Intelligence Community Whistle-blower Protection Act, Drake complained to his bosses, the NSA Inspector General, the Defence Department Inspector General, and both the House and Senate Congressional Intelligence Committees. Through official channels, Drake addressed multi-billion-dollar frauds within the NSA as well as significant intelligence failures, and it wasn't until after exhausting all these options in 2006 that he made what he calls a 'fateful decision' to go to the press with what he knew.

2006 wasn't the best time for such leaks as a large-scale security investigation was underway in the light of an article by James Risen and Eric Lichtblau. This article, published in December 2005, had let the world know for the first time that in the wake of September 11th 2001, President George W. Bush (one of the best stand-up comics ever who ever ended up in politics) had secretly authorised the National Security Agency to listen in to Americans and others inside the United States, crucially without the court-issued warrants normally required. Although Risen and Lichtblau wrote a series of investigative reports about the Agency's surveillance of international communications and about a package called the Terrorist Finance Tracking Program, which involved searches of money transfer records in the international SWIFT database, these articles took about a year to appear as they were subject to constant requests and redactions from the US government.

Drake, however, after years of attempting to use the official channels, went ahead with his releases and for doing things in the correct and proper fashion, he was charged under espionage laws, as well as for obstruction of justice and making false statements – for which he faced over 35 years in prison if he were to be found guilty on all ten felony counts. This treatment sent a chilling message that was picked up on by Edward Snowden, who chose a different tack when it came to his own revelations.

What Thomas Drake described in his descriptions of the NSA's activity pointed to fraud and violations of the constitutions, although he found it took months to get this message across to the press, who generally styled him as a threat to national security. Thomas Drake now looks back upon a very different life, and has given many interviews describing how he was victimised by the country whose Constitution he had taken an oath to uphold:

> I now tell people that before you decide to blow the whistle or leak to the press in the public interest, make sure you hire a really good attorney

or an advocacy or support group. Life is going to change in ways you may not have fully imagined or appreciated. In some ways, I've acknowledged I'm a case study in this. It comes back to 'Why did you do it?' Well, all of this is being done under the mantle of national security. All of this is being done ostensibly for us to keep us safe, but we don't know about it, not debating it and not being informed. For me, it came down to, after four-plus years of threats, how far the government gave itself extraordinary license to do whatever it felt like. And I decided to take a stand.

(Al Jazeera, 12th November 2015)

The illustrious history of whistle-blowing indeed proves that little changes. The other great precursor to Edward Snowden and Thomas Drake is Daniel Ellsberg, the former RAND Corporation military analyst who, along with Anthony Russo, leaked the Pentagon Papers, a secret account of the Vietnam War, to the *New York Times* in 1971. These documents revealed long-term practices of deception by previous administrations, and significantly contributed to the erosion of public support for the war in Vietnam. The Pentagon Papers release also triggered a legal case concerning government efforts to prevent the publication of classified information that was heard by the US Supreme Court – and much as Edward Snowden is vilified by our current administration, Ellsberg was the subject of retaliation by the government of his day. In this instance, a covert group known as The White House Plumbers, which included CIA personnel, was established by Richard Nixon. This team, on their boss's instructions, broke into Ellsberg's psychiatrist's office in an effort to find potentially embarrassing information – an operation which failed.

If any curious readers have been wondering what the difference between a leaker and whistle-blower is, then some clues have been left by the press in reporting these tales of mettle and good-conscience. Thus it is that we saw in the case of Thomas Drake, the media arguing that Drake was not a whistle-blower on wrongdoing but a leaker who threatened security. There lies the difference. Whistle-blowers expose violations of law, and abuses of authority and so forth, while leakers are styled as doing the same but with villainous intentions. It is of course lawful for a whistle-blower-leaker to disclose information confidentially to any audience if the information is not classified or specifically prohibited by statute – and so under most circumstances, there is no difference between a leaker and a whistle-blower. When you are soaking up your news from your favourite outlet however, do bear this distinction in mind. The emphasis between whistle-blowers and leakers is on whether you are, in the eyes of the public, a good person or a bad one. This is a debate that runs constant in these pages. All of the individuals mentioned in this context are held by some to be heroes while others call them traitors and criminals, a conversation that finds its ultimate expression in Edward Snowden, whom we'll turn to shortly. In the meantime, we could safely say that if the war on privacy hasn't been already lost, it is certainly a one-sided battle that many of us have chosen to ignore. This may be because the issues and implications are too large and it may be because the proliferation and technological sophistication presented creates the impression that we are powerless and this data collection is the plain corollary of the information age.

The phrase 'bulk personal datasets', coined by the UK government in 2015, speaks volumes about the new world into which we are slipping. What this phrase refers to are large compilations of data containing personally identifiable information on a large number of individuals, and the problem now is not so much whether they should: or not be collected, but what to do with them, how to protect them and what their legal status may be. These datasets exist because of mass surveillance in the United Kingdom and citizens around the world, and all large government bodies possess them.

In dealing with our bulk personal datasets the UK government passed the Investigatory Powers Act 2016, which went into force on the last day of that year and is more commonly known as the Snooper's Charter. The legislation within the Act is for state benefit solely and the provisions within it offer zero comfort for users, Internet companies, or service providers. In brief, the Investigatory Powers Act 2016 gives greater power to government to access and listen in on encrypted communications used across smart devices and computers, and if you require an image of that to dwell upon, imagine Theresa May's sad vampiric frontage watching you and your friends for signs of terrorism, everywhere you go. A short description of the logic of the act might argue that Internet censorship is going to be put in place to stop terrorism, but the consequences and culminations of the act are far worse.

For example, the act also seems to allow the police and intelligence agencies to carry out what they call 'targeted equipment interference' – what you would probably describe as hacking into your computer – and among other things it also appears to allow 48 government authorities, including the Police Service, the Air Force, the Home Office and the Foods Standard Agency warrantless access to your browsing history. If this is true, and I suspect it is, I find myself wondering again why we are not going down fighting, why this disempowerment leads to debility, and why decreasing personal power is something so many are content to vote for?

My own wonderings aside, the Snooper's Charter is the most recent front opened in Britain's war on privacy. The bill finds its immediate roots in 2000, when the British Labour Party enacted the Regulation of Investigatory Powers Act (RIPA), which became the central legal framework governing surveillance. RIPA granted surveillance powers and data access rights to public agencies while simultaneously, there was a growth in the use of CCTV by public authorities – Britain as you already know is infamous for its cameras. RIPA was also the legal framework within which the UK police used surveillance capabilities.

After the 7th July 2005 London bombings, Prime Minister Tony Blair proposed the long-term storage of telecommunications traffic data for all British citizens, and in 2006, the Identity Cards Act was introduced, although it was later repealed in 2010.

In its first appearance, the Snooper's Charter did have a catchy if uninspiring name – DRIP. The Data Retention and Investigatory Powers Act 2014 (also called DRIPA) allowed security services access to the phone and Internet records of individuals and was interpreted by Open Rights Group and Liberty as being an infringement of privacy. Following legal action in July 2015, the High Court issued an order that sections 1 and 2 of the Act were unlawful, and the alternative legislation, which became the Investigatory Powers Bill, came into effect at the beginning of 2017.

It's the unexpected set of new powers in the Bill that have upset citizens and activists, most especially the powers which have been included which allow our government bodies to collect the browsing records of everyone in the UK and have them read by a variety of authorities. In the bill there are also new ways to force companies and organisations to hand over data that they have about people to intelligence agencies, and contrary to what the government's useful idiots may tell us, this now means that a good percentage of the UK working population can now potentially look up each other's information.

The 'potentially' part of the process is of interest, because while Reddit argues about what will and will not be possible when the powers come to be, the message from 10 Downing Street and the British Home Office is roughly as follows: Don't attend protests, don't visit websites critical of the government, don't visit websites critical of the police, don't visit whistle-blowing sites, don't visit any site that covers material the government considers 'stolen' - WikiLeaks, the Intercept, etc, don't visit sites of non-conservative political parties, don't visit sites known to harbour 'esoteric content' like 4chan, don't look up health, sex, relationship or legal advice, and don't search for anything you wouldn't be happy for your partner, parents, and employer to know about.

'Does the UK really want the dubious honour of introducing powers deemed too intrusive by all other major democracies, joining the likes of China and Russia in collecting everyone's browsing habits?' said Anne Jellema, the head of the World Wide Web Foundation (Bloomberg, 11th February 2016)

It is hard to find positive comment of any sort concerning the Act, but it does have its defenders. The director general of MI5, Andrew Parker, did give a rare interview to *The Guardian* (1st November 2016) in which he offered a cold yet confident spin on the intrusive capabilities of the act, saying: 'It is vital to me that in the Internet age we are able to look at the data to find these people who mean this country harm.' The legal logic lies in the possibility that to capture any malefactor, we must all sacrifice our privacy. Andrew Parker proves this when he says: 'To find and stop the people who threaten the UK, we need to be able to monitor the communications of terrorists and spies and others who threaten the country.' To which he adds: 'Security officials have long insisted that the proliferation of encryption on apps on phones and in online communications is a godsend for terrorists.'

Similarly, Home Secretary Amber Rudd, who was famously jeered at by rank and file police when she reiterated that old Tory claim that 'the British Conservatives were the party of law and order,' claimed that the legislation was needed to protect 'the country's national security', and called the IPA 'world-leading legislation that provides unprecedented transparency and substantial privacy protection'.

Adding to this piss-poor parade of precepts, Alex Younger, the head of MI6, said that the Investigatory Powers Act provides British intelligence services with the legality needed to 'battle the existential threat' brought by data and Internet (telegraph.co.uk, 20th September 2016). Briefly unpacking that statement, we find a mind-set that sees the very existence of the Internet as problematic, and realise that we are dealing with an armed and dangerous ruling class that seeks first and foremost only to provide a call to arms in controlling it.

Similar legislation or discussions exist in other

countries. For example, in the Netherlands, on 14th February 2017, the Intelligence and Security Services Act was passed by the lower house, allowing intelligence services to have broader powers for bulk data collection, rather than using a more targeted approach. Like the UK Act, there is a 'double-lock' – many powers require a 'sign-off' from the Minister of the Interior and a review committee. Rob Bertholee, head of the General Intelligence and Security Service of the Netherlands, says that this law is necessary as the 'threat [to national security] hasn't been this high in years'.

In France, a surveillance law was rushed through in 2015. However, in October 2016, it was ruled unconstitutional by the French Constitutional Council, as a 'key clause essentially allowed security agencies to monitor and control wireless communications without the usual oversight applied to wireless operations'. The Council had concerns that the bulk collection of data would identify, without authorisation, individual conversations and communications. Further, the law did not contain definitions of the surveillance and control measures it would have enabled or allowed.

In the United States, on 15th February 2017, the Geolocation Privacy and Surveillance Act was passed, requiring law enforcement agencies to obtain a warrant before using GPS data to track an individual's location, and service providers to get customer consent before sharing geolocation data with outside agencies. PRISM, the National Security Agency's electronic surveillance programme exposed by Edward Snowden, gathers messaging data from major technology companies 'sent to and from a foreign object under surveillance' – and it also incidentally collects data 'during communication with a target reasonably believed to be living overseas', without a warrant. Section 702 of the Foreign Intelligence Surveillance Act (1973) officially 'accommodates US surveillance of foreign targets abroad', but can be used to 'collect emails, instant messages and the browsing histories of the individuals it targets – and anyone who talks to them'.

Arguing that the British Investigatory Powers Act was taking things too far, major global technology and telecommunications companies, from Microsoft to Google to Vodafone, raised their objections. Interestingly, Facebook, Google, Microsoft, Twitter and Yahoo all joined to present suggestions and substantive arguments against the act (data.parliament.uk, Written Evidence IPB0116) in which they said: 'The actions the UK Government takes here could have far reaching implications – for our customers, for your own citizens, and for the future of the global technology industry.'

What was fascinating here was that before they inevitably capitulated, these tech giants were arguing that the consequences of the act as they saw it would be a loss of user trust. Further, the same written evidence argued that this legislation would hereafter be copied around the world, and that chaos would emerge in legal disputes that cross borders. The same document reminds the UK government that bulk data collection is not permitted internationally, or even nationally by themselves and by their own legal system, and that the language in the bill does not even allow members of the public to understand the limitations and properties of the bill, and therefore their own legal position.

Apple also submitted evidence against the act in the form of an eight-page document, in which they stated the implications for their own company and user base, as well for the population as a whole. Their document quoted on bbc.co.uk (21st December 2015) said:

> • 'We owe it to our customers to protect their personal data to the best of our ability. Increasingly stronger – not weaker – encryption is the best way to protect against these threats.'
> • 'The bill threatens to hurt law-abiding citizens in its effort to combat the few bad actors who have a variety of ways to carry out their attacks. The creation of back doors and intercept capabilities would weaken the protections built into Apple products and endanger all our customers. A key left under the doormat would not just be there for the good guys. The bad guys would find it too.'
> • 'By mandating weakened encryption in Apple products, this bill will put law-abiding citizens at risk, not the criminals, hackers and terrorists who will continue having access to encryption.'

- 'The bill would also force companies to expend considerable resources hacking their own systems at the government's direction. This mandate would require Apple to alter the design of our systems and could endanger the privacy and security of users in the UK and elsewhere. We are committed to doing everything in our power to create a safer and more secure world for our customers. But it is our belief this world cannot come by sacrificing personal security.'

All of these are of course fairly decent arguments, and it is a pity that Apple didn't use anything more than an 8-page letter to act on their concerns. Instead, it is left to the activists. Open Rights Group's Executive Director, Jim Killock, described the act in November 2016 as one of the most extreme surveillance laws ever passed in a democracy, and he believes that other countries (especially those with poor human rights records) will use the legislation to justify their own intrusive surveillance programmes. The Open Rights Group have consistently opposed this bill, organising letters to be sent to MPs and under the banner Privacy, not PRISM, they have previously brought a case to the European Court of Human Rights. They have a dedicated Campaigns Hub online, for resources regarding their work against this bill, found at openrightsgroup.org.

The Institute of Advanced Legal Studies, in February 2017, published a report titled 'Protecting Sources and Whistle-blowers in a Digital Age' which stated that it was harder for journalists to protect sources due to the Investigatory Powers Act. Tom Watson MP and David Davis, in July 2015, brought a legal challenge to the European Court of Justice regarding 'the legality of GCHQ's bulk interception of call records and online messages', and were supported by Liberty, the Law Society, the Open Rights Group and Privacy International. While this went ahead the campaign group Liberty launched a crowd-funded legal challenge in January 2017, seeking a High Court judicial review. Their fundraising target was raised in less than a week, and they have sought High Court permission to proceed, as of March 2017. The Director of Liberty stated:

> Last year, this government exploited fear and distraction to quietly create the most extreme surveillance regime of any democracy in history. Hundreds of thousands of people have since called for this Act's repeal because they see it for what it is – an unprecedented, unjustified assault on our freedom.

The organisation plans to challenge the lawfulness of the following:

> • Police and agencies having access to electronic devices like computers, phones and tablets 'on an industrial scale, regardless of whether their

owners are suspected of involvement in crime – leaving them vulnerable to further attack by hackers';

• The state being able to read 'texts, online messages and emails and listen in on calls en masse, without requiring suspicion of criminal activity';

• The forcing of communications companies and service providers to 'hand over records of everybody's emails, phone calls and texts and entire web browsing history to state agencies to store, data-mine and profile at its will';

• The enabling of agencies to acquire and link databases held by the public or private sector, which can contain 'details on religion, ethnic origin, sexuality, political leanings and health problems, potentially on the entire population – and are ripe for abuse and discrimination' (all from liberty-human-rights.org.uk).

Meanwhile, I turn to a series of browser plug-ins, virtual private networks and other suspicious sounding ploys, some of which I will list in this volume, in order to keep my computer and my phone as private as possible. Not only is this increasingly hard but it does slow down my day, as well as my machines, and it reminds me again of this commonly touted question: what have I got to hide, anyway?

The other question of course, is how did such a mess of mass-applied lunacy pass through parliamentary debate or national approval?

The answer is of course that it didn't. The powers that are here described have been enabled through loopholes in the Regulation of Investigatory Powers Act (2000) which, as I said, was pushed in under Tony Blair's New Labour government, and which have enabled the secret state to intercept and store data via fibre-optic cables, all of which is aided by what looks like a blatant network of corrupted human beings looking the other way.

As reported in *The Guardian* (21st June 2013) one of GCHQ's senior legal advisers (whom the newspaper would not name) commented in light of the UK's spying agencies democratic accountability: 'We have a light oversight regime compared with the US'.

In the meantime, I can keep asking myself, as you must too: what do I have to hide? It's a question we'll return to soon.

CHAPTER 3 COLLECT IT ALL – THE CASE OF EDWARD SNOWDEN

> Arguing that you don't care about the right to privacy because you have nothing to hide is no different than saying you don't care about free speech because you have nothing to say.
>
> Edward Snowden on Reddit, 2015

Having seen that Thomas Drake tried every possible channel open to him, Edward Snowden probably felt that he had no choice but to leave the United States forever to blow the whistle.

The bones of Edward Snowden's story and the reasons for his actions are well recorded in Glenn Greenwald's book *No Place to Hide: Edward Snowden, the NSA, and the Surveillance State* (2014). From the moment he declared himself to the world, however, Edward Snowden has said that he wished more than anything for people to focus on the material he offered, and to debate the evidence rather than to discuss himself, his personality and motivations.

In respecting that there is little to add to Snowden's biography, we'll restrict ourselves to the basics. The primary details are, then, that Edward Snowden, born in 1983, worked for the CIA and then with Booz Allen Hamilton, an NSA contractor. On May 20, 2013, Snowden flew to Hong Kong after leaving his job at an NSA facility in Hawaii and shortly after that he revealed thousands of classified NSA documents to journalists Glenn Greenwald, Laura Poitras and Ewen MacAskill. Once the material had been examined, stories appeared in *The Guardian* and the *Washington Post*, and further disclosures were made by other newspapers including *Der Spiegel* and the *New York Times* – a process which continues, even if the initial impact of the files has waned.

As a consequence of Edward Snowden's releases, a public debate sprung up, a debate that was as widespread and as piqued as the disputes of the 1770s, when the British launched their Writs of Assistance. Unlike the American Revolution however, the controversy Edward Snowden kicked off remains unfinished and concerns not just the suspicion, but the confirmation that for whatever reasons, our governments (through the NSA and the GCHQ) are monitoring all our communications. By 'all our communications' this in fact means all Internet traffic, mobile communication networks, as well as routine spying on businesses, governments and intergovernmental organisations such as the United Nations. Insofar as this, Edward Snowden's work has been a success – thanks to him and his predecessors, every citizen is at least aware of the issues of and probably has an opinion on mass surveillance. Most will know how powerless we are in the face of this, and in purchasing computers and mobile devices, we are all now aware that the technology we thrive on is a two-edged instrument. As there is no sign that the technology shows any sign of slowing, it stands to reason that the issue will remain so long as the automation extends.

Technology gets better, humans do not.
anonymous

Although the monitoring of communication is the part we hear most about, much of the work of our signals intelligence organisations do is in sifting and assessing the utility of their captured data. From time to time it is wise to consider their own goals, and ask what is going on. In the formulation of Sir David Omand, a former British intelligence chief, the goal of the intelligence service is 'for citizens to trust the state to manage the threats to their everyday lives.' (*The Economist*, 12th November 2016). According to Julian Assange, however, who is another type of expert, 'democracies are always lied into war,' and the intelligence services are active in playing their part in this.

'What is in the big media machine?' he adds. 'It's the various institutions that get too comfortable and too close to the table of power, the very table that they are meant to be reporting on and policing, and getting into the historical record.' In discussing, for example, DreamWorks' feature film about WikiLeaks itself, *The Fifth Estate* (Bill Condon, 2013), Assange added: 'There are mechanisms of propaganda which go under the surface, they are not direct factual claims, and those are things like Hollywood movies.' Having read a leaked draft of the script, Assange described this feature film during a presentation of the Sam Adams Award for Integrity in Intelligence, as a 'serious propaganda attack on WikiLeaks and the integrity of its staff', as a 'lie built upon a lie', and as 'fanning the flames for war on Iran'. (Julian Assange at Sam Adams Awards, Corrente, 17th March 2013).

Although the Internet presents untold opportunities for surveillance, it is not a declared fact that intelligence agencies are plotting mass public scrutiny, although in a way the idea does provide a general benefit to law and order. There are few countries which actually seek to talk about their intelligence as it is, and unlike Russia and China, where untrammelled public surveillance is the norm, Great Britain and the United States have public systems of oversight and many politicians and rights groups which speak up against abuses and unjust practises.

Internet and mobile security is only as good as the amount of money and hours you can apply to it, and so having well-funded agencies employing thousands of experts means that many varieties of analysis are possible. Some of the data handling techniques used by the NSA and the GCHQ are experimental, while others are even among the greatest innovations in the Internet. Of course, state information security has always gone on and we cannot say we were not warned. The American intelligence community has always been at the forefront of advances in networked computing, and they even helped build the forerunners to our modern Internet and, during Nixon's time, experimented with ARPANET (the packet-switched precursor to the Internet we use today) for such purposes.

Although we don't know for certain, it is estimated that there are included in the total Edward Snowden cache at least 58,000 British intelligence files, about 1.7 million US intelligence files, and at least 15,000 Australian intelligence files. As a contractor of the NSA, Snowden had access to US government documents along with top secret files belonging to several allied governments, via the exclusive Five Eyes network. For the time being, Snowden also claims that he is not in physical possession of any of these documents, having surrendered all copies to the journalists he met in Hong Kong, and similarly, and according to his lawyer, Snowden has said that he will not release any further documents himself, leaving the responsibility for any other disclosures solely to journalists.

Before looking at some of the programs discussed by Edward Snowden in more detail, here are a few of the more staggering eye-openers which emerged from Snowden's 2013-2016 work:

1. From Edward Snowden's releases, we saw how secret court orders from FISA allow the NSA to sweep up Americans' phone records.
2. We learned that through the project called PRISM, US tech giants like Google, Facebook,

Microsoft and Apple are compelled by law to comply with requests for any desired data.

3. The GCHQ, we discovered, taps fibre-optic cables all over the world to observe and store data on the move. The GCHQ works closely with, and is funded by the NSA, and together they share data through a program called TEMPO-RA, which allows them to collect large amounts of data partly in collaboration with some named companies, which include British Telecommunications and Vodafone Cable.

4. Many were surprised to learn that the NSA and GCHQ spy on world leaders, the most high-profile revelation being that they spied on the phone of German Chancellor Angela Merkel. In fact, and based on the disclosures, the German news outlet *Der Spiegel* reported that the NSA targets at least 122 world leaders.

5. Through Edward Snowden's files, private Internet users learned for the first time of XKEY-SCORE, a program that sees everything a person does on the Internet, through data that is intercepted all over the world. One of the documents the NSA produced describes XKEYSCORE as the 'widest-reaching' system to search through Internet data. Snowden's NSA releases show that XKEYSCORE can track down single users based on metrics such as race, sex, ethnicity, and location. On January 26, 2014, the German broad-

caster Norddeutscher Rundfunk asked Edward Snowden what he could do with this program. He answered: 'You could read anyone's email in the world, anybody you've got an email address for. Any website – you can watch traffic to and from it. Any computer that an individual sits at – you can watch it. Any laptop that you're tracking – you can follow it as it moves from place to place throughout the world. It's a one-stop-shop for access to the NSA's information.'

6. It was revealed that the NSA has a series of techniques to circumvent web encryption technologies. These include forcing companies like Microsoft to install backdoors in their software, hacking into servers and individual computers, or promoting the use of weaker encryption technologies.

7. We found that the NSA has its own elite hacker team codenamed Tailored Access Operations (TAO) that can break into computers anywhere and infect them with malware when other surveillance tactics fail.

8. When bulk collection of data or PRISM fails, it was shown that the agencies could infiltrate the connections between Yahoo and Google data centres, an exposure that was made famous by a PowerPoint slide that celebrated this fact with a smiley face. This story angered the tech companies in question and all of them announced plans

to strengthen and encrypt those links to avoid this kind of surveillance.

9. Snowden's Global Surveillance Files showed how the NSA collects many of the world's text messages, easily grabbing 200 million every day through a program called DISHFIRE. In another document, this was described as a 'goldmine to exploit' for many separate varieties of personal data. It appears that the NSA has used this database to extract information on people's travel plans, contact books, financial transactions and more – including the details of individuals under no suspicion of illegal activity.

10. Also, we learned that NSA had been intercepting every single phone call in the Bahamas and Afghanistan through a program called MYSTIC, as well as collecting every single item of phone metadata for Mexico, Kenya and the Philippines. This, as well as the heavy monitoring of Latin America, was elaborated upon by Julian Assange in a *The Guardian* article (9th July 2013): 'Mass surveillance is not just an issue for democracy and governance,' he said, 'it's a geopolitical issue. The surveillance of a whole population by a foreign power naturally threatens sovereignty. Intervention after intervention in the affairs of Latin American democracy have taught us to be realistic. We know that the old powers will still exploit any advantage to delay or suppress the outbreak of Latin American independence.'

Readers are encouraged to dip into the capacious and seemingly limitless amount of files that Edward Snowden has made public, and there is an excellent searchable database of the material online – and no – it is not illegal to access it. You can read it all right now and in fact, Edward Snowden has made his data accessible, user-friendly and organised. As a responsible whistle-blower, Edward Snowden has redacted his data where necessary, and is certain that the information he is sharing is of the highest public interest, and that its release does not endanger the lives of any British, American or other people.

Snowden's files can be found at the address search.edwardsnowden.com where you will discover a varied selection of material that is fairly comprehensible to almost anybody, and sometimes even entertaining as it includes cheesy PowerPoint style graphics, and quite readable descriptions of the multitudinous programs devised in order to indiscriminately copy and record everything, from shopping, to keywords, to keystrokes, to some scandalous phone-tapping and high level government and industrial reconnaissance.

All this data was therefore published in the public interest, although at the outset there was only one piece of information that the authorities cared about – Snowden's identity and location – and as soon as he revealed this, his pursuit and prosecution began.

Thus it was that on 21st June 2013, the US Department of Justice unsealed charges against Snowden on two counts of violating the Espionage Act of 1917 and theft of US government property. Following that, on June 23rd, Snowden flew to Moscow where the Russian authorities later granted him an asylum period that was later extended to three years – and as of 2017, he is still living in an undisclosed location in Russia while seeking asylum elsewhere.

In the meantime, Edward Snowden has released a well-selected trove of documents which will serve journalists, bloggers and analysts for a long time – and how incredible that through Snowden's actions, every person, even those uninterested in these issues, will now know what they have perhaps long suspected – that it is all collected. This is a reference to what Glenn Greenwald called 'the crux of the NSA story in one phrase'. The phrase 'collect it all' as reported, has been attributed to General Keith Alexander – 16th Director of the National Security Agency – who took the approach that instead of looking for a needle in a haystack, his agency and the GCHQ should simply scoop up the entire haystack.

Hence – 'Collect it all, tag it, store it... And whatever it is you want, you go searching for it.' (General Keith Alexander, quoted in *The Washington Post*, 15th July 2013).

Since 2013, then, it has been impressive just how much work Snowden has provided not for journalists but for interested citizens.

Look at his files and you will read about BULL-RUN, an NSA program allegedly named after an American Civil War battle, just as its UK version, EDGEHILL, is named after an English Civil War battle. The reason these programs were named with civil war in mind, Snowden believes, is because they target domestic infrastructure. This is because BULLRUN and EDGEHILL are programs through which the NSA and GCHQ are said to intentionally mislead corporate partners, by giving what is in effect bad advice, in order to degrade the security of these corporation's services.

By these means, it is seen in Edward Snowden's documents that successive administrations are building back doors into the world's communication networks that are technically available to anyone with the resources to find them. Given that these exploits are available, this is uncommonly dangerous. It is not inconceivable for example that the TalkTalk hack of 2015 had something to do with a weakness in the system left as a part of EDGEHILL, simply because if weaknesses are to be integrated in security systems for the benefit of one party, they will be there for all with the know-how to exploit them.

One thing that seems clear is that BULLRUN targeted the Internet's most common security feature, SSL – Secure Sockets Layer. The fundamental benefit of SSL is that it provides web users with (among other things) secure shopping and banking environments – but most of us will recognise it simply as the letter 's' which marks the difference between a web address headed http:// – an unencrypted and therefore unsafe connection – and https:// – an encrypted connection.

What is sad about the GCHQ working to make SSL weaker is not their motives, but the fact that if public faith were to wane in SSL, sweeping damage would likely befall world commerce. Without faith in SSL, people would not access their banks online, and nor in fact would they want to shop as freely as they currently do on the Internet. This is because, as we must remember, a security weakness, no matter how well implemented, will remain a security soft-spot for all.

In Snowden's archive we also read about TUR-MOIL, which is what is termed a 'passive interception system', which covers the whole planet. This NSA program operates with what you may like to imagine as data sensors, which examine everything that passes their way, the presumption being they are searching for something actionable. Journalist and security researcher Jacob Appelbaum likened TURMOIL to the above-mentioned General Writ of Assistance of 1767, as both appear to be an all-encompassing and warrantless right to look into the private affairs of citizens.

There is a program called TURBINE, which, it is said, injects packets of code into passing data, in order to try and effect attacks, and some of the programs revealed, like AIRGAP, represent significant technological achievements. Formerly, it was believed that if your computer was not online, your data was safe because it could not be relayed to the Internet, but thanks to the genius of the NSA this sense of security should never be felt again! The technology of AIRGAP, as reported in the *New York Times*, has been used by the agency for several years. This arch hack uses radio waves that are transmitted from tiny circuit boards and USB cards inserted covertly into the computers. The NSA calls the effort an 'active defence' and according to documents released, it has been used to monitor the Chinese army, the Russian military, drug cartels, and trade institutions inside the European Union.

Business institutions and corporations are also of interest to the NSA and the GCHQ. One file given by Edward Snowden to *The Guardian* journalist Glenn Greenwald describes a program called BLACKPEARL, which pulls data from private networks, such as those of large companies. The private networks that appear to have been accessed include those of the Brazilian petrol giant Petrobras, the Swift network for global bank transfers, the French Foreign Ministry and Google.

If examination of the NSA files makes a person feel either too paranoid or depressed, they can always turn to examination of the macho minds behind the agency's programs, by studying the boggling array of virile and muscular titles given to the programs, and the references they make.

One of the slides in the files talks about an NSA system called SKYNET – which is the name of the all-seeing psychopathic machine enemy in the film *The Terminator* (James Cameron, 1984). The GCHQ's SKYNET uses a system of data analysis called CINEPLEX to determine what are known as 'pattern-of-life and travel-analytics' – the aim being to identify suspect activity. The SKYNET program can also, it is said, respond to such questions as: 'Who travels to or from Peshawar every second Sunday and *somewhere else* on a weekly basis.' These can combine with other questions, all concerned with travel data, relationships, and locations of people and devices of interest.

Concerning the legality of what the spooks at the NSA and GCHQ were doing, we can look no further than a program called CYBERTRANS – another crucially cocky and potent title. CYBERTRANS, it appears, was among the programs used at the agencies' Content Extraction Centre, which pulled items of interest from their mass of digital assets. Documents appear to show that British spies kept records on the employees of several German companies and that they'd infiltrated their networks to do so. One GCHQ paper claims the agency sought 'development of in-depth knowledge of key satellite IP service providers in Germany'. To achieve this, the documents show that the GCHQ had monitored German service companies and their employees and had even stolen customer lists.

Although the NSA have been hogging all the limelight and bad publicity, Britain's GCHQ is equally deserving of attention and Edward Snowden's papers appear to show that they too operate their own intrusive and probably illegal spying systems, one of which is even named after a Radiohead song – KARMA POLICE.

As Ryan Gallagher reported in *The Intercept* in September 2015, while KARMA POLICE shows GCHQ was collecting billions of Internet records every day from users all around the world, they used the program known as MUTANT BROTH to match the IP addresses in the raw data to actual users, based on information from on-browser cookies they had intercepted. One leaked document (an event log for a so-called OPERATION HIGHLAND FLING) states that Facebook cookies are especially helpful in allowing MUTANT BROTH to glean information about users. This makes perfect sense. Facebook has evolved as the ultimate identifier of who we are, and like so many other technologies, cannot be resisted when it comes to those with an urge to abuse. It looks like, according to these authorities, the Data Protection Act 1998 does not apply to them, and why should it? It is in the nature of those who have power to seek to maintain and reinforce it. Anonymisation (which is what happens when your data is collected) is the process of turning data into a form that does not identify individuals. In turn, this allows for a much wider use of the information and the Data Protection Act controls how organisations use personal data, although this does not obviously apply to the security services, who according to what we've just seen, proceed according to their own whims.

Without public interest, Edward Snowden's work may yet still have been in vain, and although there may have been a spike in awareness due to his initial revelations, the general appetite for privacy has since appeared to have faded. There is a group in the UK called the UK Anonymisation Network (UKAN), which was established for the benefit of data organisations and was intended to lead public discussion relating to anonymisation. The group exists to share best practice and protect consumer interest, but since interest in Snowden has waned, and public opinion has shifted, UKAN now display an underfunded website, which has not been updated since 2016 and a Twitter account with a meagre 200 followers. This is a reflection of how little importance we currently place on these issues, which will inevitably discomfit our children's generation.

By 2010, and according to Snowden's documents, GCHQ was indiscriminately logging 30 billion metadata records per day, and by 2012 that collection had increased to 50 billion per day, and work was going on to double that amount to 100 billion. This was what GCHQ referred to as 'population-scale' data mining, monitoring all communications across entire countries and then attempting to establish suspicious behaviours.

It might do well to interrupt here and remind ourselves of the uses of metadata, or 'data about data' to be etymologically accurate, which is gathered to identify trends, administer algorithmic solutions, and model potential behaviours. It has been said by supporters of such indiscriminate undercover activities that we shouldn't worry about being snooped upon; since most of the data collection does not include the actual content of our communications, the threat to privacy is said to be small. But this is misleading, and I will leave it to David Cole (*New York Review of Books*, 10th May 2014) who explains the difference very well:

> As NSA General Counsel Stewart Baker has said, 'metadata absolutely tells you everything about somebody's life. If you have enough metadata, you don't really need content.' When I quoted Baker at a recent debate at Johns Hopkins University, my opponent, General Michael Hayden, former director of the NSA and the CIA, called Baker's comment 'absolutely correct,' and raised him one, asserting, 'We kill people based on metadata.'

Metadata then, is just as lethal as content, and it is of course easier to collect, whether you are an ISP scooping up audience propensities to sell or a spy agency.

As far as these spy agencies go, they operate many such eavesdropping systems, each as above with its own asinine name. To wit I cite SOCIAL ANTHROPOID, which analyses metadata on emails, instant messenger chats and social media conversations; MEMORY HOLE, which records queries entered into search engines and links each search with an IP address; MARBLED GECKO, which examines searches made on Google Maps and Google Earth; and INFINITE MONKEYS, which attempts to bring meaning to the large amount of data collected from online bulletin boards and forums. The slightly disgustingly titled program DEMONSPIT is a system of dataflow for bulk call collection of calls made to and from Pakistan, and was the software which helped falsely identify Ahmad Muaffaq Zaidan, Al Jazeera's Islamabad bureau chief, as a member of the terrorist groups Al Qaeda and the Muslim Brotherhood. It is concerning to think that allowing computers to assert affiliation based on data such as phone records can allow senior journalists like Ahmad Muaffaq Zaidan to be declared as terrorists.

In response to this allegation, Al Jazeera America wrote: 'This is how America's intelligence apparatus with its massive funding, cutting-edge computers and armies of big-brained analysts identifies enemies of the state? Is it any wonder that so many civilians have been accidentally killed in drone attacks?' (15th May 2015)

Another sheep-headedly named NSA program discussed in Snowden's files is DISHFIRE, which astonished many with its daily sweep of the world's text messages, and which is ultimately aimed at capturing all the 5.3 billion mobile devices in the world. This includes data extracted concerning location, contacts, contact networks and credit card details as well as the SMS messages themselves. This content extraction targets millions, if not billions of people who are under no suspicion of illegal activity, but aspires to a level of data control and storage that will undoubtedly at some point be an extremely valuable resource. It cannot be said at this time what this data will be used for, but so long as it exists uses will be found. The next pertinent use of this large amount of data on the citizens of the world will be in experimenting with artificial intelligence, and it is certain that these programs will have begun.

The over-collection of data is an absolute theme in the Edward Snowden disclosures, as exampled in the telephony records acquired. According to Snowden and reported in the *New York Times,* the National Security Agency is capable of recording all a foreign country's telephone calls in order to later use voice analysis software to gather intelligence and review conversations for up to a month after they have taken place.

In fact, the voice interception program, MYSTIC, began in 2009, can be used for 'retrospective retrieval,' and can replay the voices from any call without requiring that a person be identified in advance for surveillance. This points to something dystopian that stretches far beyond the borders of the UK and the USA – because this subverting of personal privacy is aimed squarely at the world, and deems to command the entire power of the Internet, something that most experts fear will be achieved.

Another program called PINWALE hit the headlines because according to the Snowden documents it habitually processed data from places such as Yahoo mailboxes and Google's private clouds. It was through this admission that people came to falsely assume that the NSA had direct access to the private servers of our most popular Internet service companies, although in an interview with Bloomberg TV in October 2013, NSA Director Keith Alexander put this to rest and said: 'I can tell you factually we do not have access to Google servers or Yahoo servers.'

And factually, Alexander's denial was truthful because the NSA did not access Google's or Yahoo's servers itself, but relied on another beefcake-sounding ultramale spy program called MUSCULAR, undertaken in collaboration with the GCHQ, which tapped into networks that link those companies' data centres. The distinction here is between data at rest – that is to say data on a private server – and data on the fly – that which is on the move on the infobahn and passing from one server to the next. What we can now assume from this is that while the NSA and the GCHQ do not break into our private user accounts, they may intercept the material as it travels the optical fibre of the Internet from one data centre to another.

TEMPORA is in fact the code name for a formerly secret computer system that is used by the British GCHQ to buffer most Internet communications that are extracted from fibre-optic cables, and it holds this information so it may be processed and searched at a later time, as and when the agencies feel necessary. This system, which became operational in the autumn of 2011, uses intercepts placed in the United Kingdom which operate, it is alleged, with the knowledge of the companies who own either the cables or the various landing stations where the Internet cables come onshore. In Britain these landing stations, which are generally unobtrusive brick buildings, are largely on the west coast, with many in Cornwall and a good few more in the north west of England and Scotland.

Glenn Greenwald, Laura Poitras, *The Guardian*, the *Washington Post* and *Der Spiegel* have been particularly good at documenting the Snowden information in a series of well-reported releases. The existence of TEMPORA was first revealed by *The Guardian* in June 2013, but there are hundreds of spy programs described in the files, many of which suffer from excessively Alpha codenames – like TWISTED PATH – STONEGHOST – HAMMERSTEIN – GILGAMESH – PARANOIDSMURF – SHOTGIANT – and STORMBREW. Some of the agencies' programs have dismally transparent names like TRAFFIC THIEF and WEB CANDID – while other programs have attempted to spy on the sexual habits of known militants, in a presumable effort to smear them when necessary. Other programs have names also appropriate to their tasks, such as the programs that were put into place to spy on players of World of Warcraft and even Angry Birds.

The will for this large-scale data collection exists somewhere, although nobody is yet ready to admit where. The National Security Agency, flush and flooded with funds, has built its Utah Data Center as a collection point, and its purpose is described as being 'to intercept, decipher, analyze and store vast swaths of the world's communications … including all forms of communication, including the complete contents of private emails, cell phone calls and Google searches.'

The unexpected conclusion every citizen must now therefore make is that everything one communicates through any traceable medium, or any record of one's existence in the electronic medium, will become the property of the US government – kind of like Buckminster Emptier described at the head of this book. You may have called him paranoid then, but as of the present time, this data collection includes faceprints – thanks to all that tagging we've been doing on Facebook – everything we have ever purchased – everything we have searched for – and so on.

The go-to NSA expert on this subject – or at least the one most willing to give an honest answer – is William Binney, a former NSA crypto-mathematician who quit the NSA after seeing that the organisation was (in his view) deliberately overlooking the privacy qualifications that were built into the Constitution. A video clip shows William Binney speaking to James Bamford of *Wired* magazine, holding his thumb and forefinger close together and saying: 'We are this far from a turnkey totalitarian state.'

During interviews on Democracy Now! in April and May 2012, Binney estimated that the NSA had intercepted 20 trillion communications transactions of Americans such as phone calls, emails, and other forms of data through a program called STELLAR WIND. This included most of the emails of US citizens. In addition the NSA now has two huge data-gathering facilities, each with three 105-foot satellite dishes, as well as their Utah data headquarters.

And Binney's stance: 'When they started violating the Constitution, I couldn't stay.'

William Binney's opinions are valuable because like Edward Snowden he speaks as an insider. Since 1985 William Binney had been working at the NSA with the explicit task of automating the construction of intelligence from data. Binney helped build rules that looked at data, and put that data together in whatever strands necessary to construct arguments. One of his aims was to show the given implications from these arguments and as with other sophisticated data workers, his ultimate goal was consistency from the computers in making their assumptions. All of this can be seen in the film *The Future of Freedom* (Richard Grove, 2015).

A 36-year veteran of America's intelligence community, William Binney resigned from his position as Director for Global Communications Intelligence (COMINT) at the National Security Agency in October 2011. As Binney worked within the NSA to predict people's future actions based on available data, he wondered if systems should not be put in place in order to maximise everybody's well-being. In resigning, William Binney didn't deny that data accumulation and surveillance should be used but he argued that within it, there should exist a process that puts people first.

At the present time then it appears that the two barriers to intrusions on privacy, the technological and the constitutional, have both been dispatched. Despite this, the US court of appeals ruled in 2015 that the bulk collection of telephone metadata is unlawful, a decision that will clear the way for larger legal challenges against the National Security Agency and the GCHQ.

Richard Ledgett is the 15th Deputy Director of the NSA and through the good auspices of TED Talks he was able to respond to some of this and he also commented on the material that Edward Snowden gave the world. Ledgett's primary argument was that Edward Snowden's material had offered 'kernels of truth and a good deal of extrapolation,' and that Snowden 'put people's lives at risk'. Further, Ledgett of the NSA argued in this same talk that since Edward Snowden's releases, terrorists, smugglers and other criminals have been observed moving away from the NSA's ability to tap their communications and he concluded that this was a direct result of Snowden's leaks. In the talk, Ledgett conceded that the NSA may have been too secretive about its operations but he still argues that it must retain secrecy regarding programs in its targeting of bad guys, as the revelations of their capability will harm their efficiency.

While Internet and mobile technology was never devised for the purposes of data collection, it turns out that it is the perfect tool for doing so. In fact, we are so used to the idea of or communications being tapped that the majority of human Internet users, and probably non-users too, are essentially comfortable with whole-sale blanket surveillance. Technically, we are told that our governments have only the right to monitor foreigners, insofar as their data passes through our jurisdiction. And technically, they cannot monitor us, and so long as we don't think about it, we can just about imagine that it is not happening.

Anti-terror procedures support this attitude, but here is another thought: are the NSA and the GCHQ surveilling[6] people they know are innocent in the hope that when one of them does commit a crime, evidence can be retrospectively unearthed? While the databases these surveillance services amass complement existing human intelligence, what is effectively happening is that our computer-based activity is being recorded by other computers, which are analysing the data for patterns and behaviours the humans are looking for.

In putting these systems into place our intelligence agencies are only doing their job; signals intelligence (SIGINT) is what we asked them to do and so they are doing it to the best of their ability. Evidence seems to suggest however that these agencies have far extended their remit and have for example hacked (as we understand it) the networks of corporations. Slides from Edward Snowden's cache back this up, showing that the

---

6 The verb *surveil*, originally a backformation of the noun *surveillance*, was long considered nonstandard, and even now is still so new to the language (the earliest instances date from the early 1960s) that some dictionaries don't include it, and your spell check might disapprove of it. But even though survey is closely related to surveillance, survey does not carry the sense of close observation, especially of one under suspicion. For this purpose *surveil* works better, so the word is a useful addition to the language.

British Network Analysis Centre was deliberately accessing Belgian Telecoms company Belgacom, without any warrant and without the company's knowledge.

There is a pattern here of making our preferred technology less secure. The argument is that the moment something becomes popular, backdoors and other hacks are applied to it. Skype is a good example, as it was developed in Europe by Swedish, Danish and Estonian developers, and began its working life as a completely encrypted, peer-to-peer communication system that was perfectly safe – if you valued privacy. However, now that Skype is American-owned it is not safe, and its encryption is compromised.

Furthermore, if communications are being recorded from within the United Nations and the European Parliament – to name two – why are the NSA looking for terrorists there? When Dilma Roussef, president of Brazil addressed the United Nations about this, she said:

> If there is no right to privacy there can be no true freedom of expression and opinion, and therefore no effective democracy. (*The Guardian,* 24th September 2013)

The public may be asked to choose whether Cathy Massiter, Annie Machon, Edward Snowden, William Binney and Thomas Drake are traitors or heroes – but they are neither. If anything they are messengers, communicating information to us about our intelligence services. The dichotomy as to whether the whistle-blower is a hero or a traitor leads to a rather false debate concerning the psychology of these individuals, when the focus must be on transparency of surveillance.

Encrypting the entire Internet would end the kind of dragnet mass surveillance we are discussing here, but this is not a politically acceptable solution that you will hear voiced in any parliament. Presumably, encrypting the entire Internet would not allow any state, or any state's partners to benefit from the kind of intelligence large-scale surveillance offers. As it stands, the NSA and the GCHQ have more power than any person or organisation on the planet, and it is in the nature of power that its holders seek to retain it.

Tellingly, NSA and GCHQ data is not generally admissible in court since it was collected in a rather umbrageous manner. So far as now, and into the future too, you will never be taken to court and have information gathered by a spy agency presented as evidence against you, but as William Binney explains, there is something along the lines of a 'planned programmed perjury policy' at play.

This is a bit different from surveilling people we know are innocent in the hope that when one of them does commit a crime, evidence can be retrospectively unearthed. It just means that there are other ways of presenting evidence. So for example, it is envisaged that when a person of interest is targeted, local police anywhere in the world could now be sent information from which they can create what is known as a 'parallel construction' to generate evidence that will in turn be admissible in a court. The thought is that the data already collected upon an individual will provide incriminating information of something – including probable cause – a fact that will then rely on normal police procedures to prosecute.

While MPs in Britain and their FVEY counterparts argue that volume data collection is key to frustrating terrorist plots, I believe that they fail to address the causes of terrorism and also run roughshod over the rights of the rest of us. A further corollary is that computerised methods of crime-prevention implicate innocent people by association, or even proximity if they happen to be using the same network or connection as a criminal. As Snowden added, the agencies in question can also derive suspicion from any innocent life, and paint anyone in the context of a wrongdoer.

Alessandro Acquisti, a Professor of Information Technology and Public Policy states that 'any personal information can be sensitive information' (Talk: *The Dark Side of Data*, December 2013). His argument is that facial data combined with the amount of photographs available and the rapid increase in abilities of facial recognised technology has literally brought everything to a head – your head.

To demonstrate this, Professor Acquisti has made a proof of concept app that returns publicly available information including a date of birth and social security information from a camera looking at a random face in a crowd. The professor's argument is that your face is a data point, from which much can then be inferred and he is justifiably proud that he has proved this using openly visible and available data. Professor Acquisti's discovery is that privacy is not about having something negative to hide, but about what people can find out about us. Now his students can point a camera into a public crowd and unearth all sorts of information about the individuals it identifies within that crowd – and these are just students doing this – not a global spy agency.

CHAPTER 4 INTERNET FOR SALE

The Pirate Bay, Kim Dotcom and the Fight for the Commercial Net

> The very powerful and the very stupid have one thing in common. Instead of changing their views to fit the facts, they try to change the facts to fit their views.
>
> Kim Dotcom

The foundational problem with copyright in light of digital privacy is not that creative people are sold short by piracy, because it sounds reasonable that musicians, games designers, filmmakers, software developers, photographers and writers should be paid for their work. The problem is that the law is effectively being written by lobbyists who are often experts from private companies, and that these laws are being pushed through voting systems in which most of the parliamentarians don't fully appreciate the issues.

Danny Hillis talks fondly of the early days of the Internet and he has every right to – he was the third person to ever register a domain name.

'I could have had anything I wanted apart from bbn.com and symbolics.com,'[7] he says, 'and so I picked

---

7 The oldest extant registered generic top-level domain used in the Domain Name System of the Internet is symbolics.com, registered on March 15, 1985. bbn.com was registered on April 24, 1985 and think.com on May 24, 1985.

think.com. But then I thought: you know, there's a lot of really interesting names out there, maybe I should register a few extras, just in case? And then I thought: nah. That wouldn't be very nice.'

If this was the spirit in the first occasions of the Internet, the network has since changed. The same Internet is now a global marketplace and technological fact that mediates working, social and political relationships. Domain names can now be worth millions and there are copious land-grabbing prospects to hand in the generic domains that are being rolled out in batches – hundreds at a time. These include domain extensions such as .yoga, .republican, .sexy, .scot, .coffee and .fish – all of which were released in one block. At the same time the Internet is the most democratic media form imaginable and for virtually no investment, anyone can have a website and almost any business can find a market.

Ownership of digital media, like ideas and data, is a privacy issue. In many cases copyright laws emulate the privacy legislation we've looked at, because they are not made by normal democratic protocols, which include transparency and oversight, but are put in place by advocates who seek to persuade members of the government to enact legislation that would benefit their group. The lobbying profession is a legitimate part of our democratic political process but it is one that is not very well understood.

Hacktivist and privacy champion Arjen Kamphuis has therefore decided to treat his respect for copyright on a case-by-case basis. This is because he feels copyright must serve society and if he sees it as serving private companies and purely profitable interests, he is not prepared to respect it.

'There is a big middle ground here,' he says, 'and what the music and movie industry have done has damaged our faith and our ability to have faith in these legal systems.'

Kamphuis's point is that laws are at best outdated, and when new laws are introduced, they are often biased. There are flaws in the belief that piracy is a completely bad thing, but in trying to deal with it our constitutions appear out of control and so a metric ton of laws have been passed so that digital media is protected.One reason for this is that digital piracy is increasingly quick, easy and accessible to everyone.

This idea of the law being at odds with technology is so universal as to almost be a principle. Taking the example of public or commercially operated drones, we find the law at a loss because like other technology, drone mechanics are often abused by criminals – dropping packages in prisons or casing prospective properties for burglary, and of course terrorism. Such drones are difficult for authorities to combat first because the access to radar technology useful for locating them is highly restricted and in the hands of the military, meaning that the radio communication between the drone and its operator is the only option for targeting them. However, intercepting signals used by a drone could be interpreted as an illegal wiretap, and jamming signals is also against the law (*The Economist,* 20th May 2016).

Listening to Arjen Kamphuis, we sense that the law will never be able to keep pace with accelerating changes. When it comes to the distribution of digital media, torrent sites are replicable and quick, while file sharing means that individual pirated items can barely be tracked. Considering this, it would seem safe to assert that traditional policing methods are not going to work, and that is why Kamphuis is one of many who suggest that copyright should be something like twelve years, as opposed to the standard 'life of author plus 75 years'. In fact when copyright came into being the original term of ownership was fourteen years – a timescale which seems all the more surprising when you consider that when this was established in the eighteenth century, technology barely moved at all. For patents, the same sort of duration may apply, and fifteen years should sound sensible to most, with perhaps there being arguments in certain areas in which it could stretch to twenty years. There is, in Kamphuis' opinion, a strong case for saying that locking up elements of science and culture for over a century in some cases does not serve society, and it is these arguments which form the ground for much of what is discussed by copyright activists today.

Even though the United Kingdom is the second worst country in the world for illegal music downloads – behind the United States – the vast majority of people don't mind supporting artists or scientific endeavour but will not be happy about buying a digital version of a song and finding that they can only play it on an approved device, such as an iPod.

It also appears that a large percentage of people have at some point or another obtained illegally copied material, but estimates vary as to how many.[8] While governments – backed by industry lobbyists – will continue to chase users and services which may be downloading or sharing pirated material, they should probably be more worried in the meantime about the fact that so many people, however many there are, have come to the conclusion that the laws are wrong.

This is why the Pirate Party started in Sweden – not because its members decided they wanted illegal downloads at the expense of copyright holders – but because a substantial body of people had concluded that the current burden of copyright laws were not fit for purpose, and in some cases even immoral. This, and the fact that the Pirate Party has won electoral seats across Europe, constitutes a difference between piracy for the sake of it, and piracy from principle. I would also suggest that the Pirate Party was the first actual international political party to win seats anywhere, as valid a fact about the modern world as may be needed at all.

The first such electoral victory was in 2009 in Sweden, where the Pirate Party of Sweden candidate

8 A MusicWatch study of 2016 (*TechTimes,* 26th February 2016) concluded from a survey of 1,000 people that 57 million Americans acquire music from unlicensed sources. I am absolutely unclear as to how these survey results are affirmed, but there are plenty of surveys to choose from and the results vary, saying that between 20% to 50% of the adult population access illegal material online.

Christian Engström was elected as the first ever Pirate Party Member of European Parliament (MEP) – and there have been similar successes in Germany. In the Berlin State Election in 2011 the Pirate Party of Berlin – a state chapter of Pirate Party Germany – won close to 9% of the vote and the lead candidate of the party list, Andreas Baum, was given a seat. This, as well as successes in Iceland, the Czech Republic and Luxembourg, should act as a reminder to the established political parties that they may be overlooking a new political movement which is aimed at what it views as the bleak evolution of global digital freedoms and copyright policy.

Broadly speaking, Pirate Parties in the 42 countries where they exist stand for civil rights, more direct participation in government, reform of copyright and patent law, the free sharing of knowledge through open systems, and information privacy. These political parties do not campaign for the right to download free films and music, but stand for an economy of the common good, and advocate a more co-operational method of government, fostering solidarity with other political parties as opposed to our more habitual confrontational politics. This puts these Pirate Parties not at odds with governments, but with the lobbyists who inform governments. Even the peerlessly sarcastic Anonymous website encyclopediadramatica.rs seems to have a grudging respect for Pirate Parties, and in Sweden, the Piratpartiet is still the third largest political party by membership.

One reason for the popularity of the world's Pirate Parties is the free software revolution, a fact of life largely taken for granted by the rest of us. So much of the software we use has been copied from other places, however, and on your own computer you will have free software that demonstrates this. Such free or open-source software is one of the mainstays of the technological revolution we are still experiencing and the open sharing of such software keeps developers interested, and is representative of the larger human collaboration which defines what some of us used to imagine would be the free spirit of the Internet. The prime example of this was the creation of the Linux operating system by Linus Torvald in 1995. Because Linus Torvald made the Linux 'kernel' free – the kernel being the lowest level of replaceable software that interfaces with all the computer's hardware, processes and applications – we live in a vastly different and improved world. The same Linux kernel runs virtually everything computer-based on the planet now, and of course it even runs applications off the planet such as the computers onboard the International Space Station, and other satellites. Just about everything in fact – web servers, cameras, televisions, cars, thermostats, aeroplanes and traffic control systems – are run on Linux – a free to share, copy and adapt operating system. Nowadays it is possible for us to use computers without knowing anything about how they work, but when the technology was being developed, especially in the 1970s and 1980s it was not this way at all. Everybody interested in computers in those days replicated, re-wrote and re-used software without a thought for copyright, and the issue of ownership only became real at the point of sale. In the same way, our computers run open source browsers, anti-virus, and device drivers that are open source, and we use these programs assuming perhaps that they are already somehow paid for, even if they are not.

The fluid nature of copying in the cyber-sphere is demonstrated in the movie *Pirates of Silicon Valley* (Martyn Burke, 1999) – although the ham-acting, sinister music and clumsy messaging leave plenty to be desired. By the definitions of intellectual property that we adhere to so closely in pursuing Internet pirates, however, we see in this movie that Steve Jobs of Apple 'stole' software, as did the developers at Microsoft. The story goes that Steve Jobs was allowed by the management at Xerox to examine the graphical interface they were working on, and it was material developed from this software that now runs on billions of devices, in the form of Windows and Apple iOS operating systems. Microsoft bought Q-DOS (Quick and Dirty Operating System) from the Seattle Computer Company for $50,000 to resell to IBM for $50 a copy, and after IBM and Microsoft signed the deal to license MS-DOS (Microsoft Disk Operating System), Bill Gates became one of the richest people in the world. Furthermore, the accusation goes that Microsoft was doing work for Apple at the time and obtained prototypes of their Apple Lisa machine, which featured the graphical operating system that Steve Jobs developed after seeing what was going on at Xerox – and from that Microsoft were able to develop Windows thereafter.

It's hard to get a complete picture of the evolution and unravelling of expertise that led to Internet, mobile and computer technology, but that's the way it should be – the events which brought about these departures were collaborative, sometimes fortuitous and did not belong to one person or set of people. What remains is that the first computers had no graphic interface whatsoever and you had to know code to get them to do anything. The icons and the point and click menus which we now use were invented at Xerox in Rochester, New York, but unfortunately it seems that at the time Xerox were not wholly aware of what an important property this was going to be.

Copying, therefore, as Peter Sunde, the founder of The Pirate Bay, recognises, is essential to human development, and it is copying, he argues, that allows technology to progress. When Sunde began to see advertisements from Hollywood that argued that copying was bad, he became involved with a group called Piratbyrån (Pirate Bureau), which was intended as a counterpoint to lobby groups such as the Swedish Anti-Piracy Bureau. The intention of the Piratbyrån was to argue that copying was a good thing and to talk about file-sharing and encourage debate and a more relaxed attitude to copying in general. The greatest project that the Piratbyrån is known for was The Pirate Bay, which is the largest file-sharing site in the world.

To be clear about this, we must understand that nobody ever downloads anything from The Pirate Bay, but instead The Pirate Bay helps users by pointing to files that are distributed across the Internet and which can be downloaded by a service called BitTorrent. What so-called 'torrent' software does is allow files to be stored and shared over many thousands of computers, and so large files can be assembled through taking various pieces of them from all over an established network of users.

Naturally, The Pirate Bay began to receive many cease and desist letters from American companies – letters that they responded to with images of polar bears. At the time of this cat and mouse game, other sites such as Supernova had already closed down under legal threats, but The Pirate Bay decided to carry on, and did so on the basis that their site was in all probability legal – although what was lacking was any precedent to show this. Early trials such as that against the Russian website AllOfMP3 were not conclusive, and cases failed generally because laws varied from territory to territory. During this scandal there was even a period during which Internet service providers in Europe could be sued if they allowed their users access to this site. The logic was that if you as an Internet Service Provider allowed copyrighted material to travel through your cables, you were infringing that copyright. This claim may have presented an underlying logic for some, but it is the sort of logic that caused one-time-United States Senator Ted Stevens to say that the Internet was in fact 'a series of tubes'. The 'series of tubes' metaphor has rightly been ridiculed, particularly because it displays a highly circumscribed and idiotic understanding of the Internet – made more ridiculous because at the time Senator Stevens had authored the Communications, Consumer's Choice, and Broadband Deployment Act of 2006 – the intention of which was to regulate the Internet.

One issue with AllOfMP3's legality was that it was licensed in Russia by the Russian Organization for Multimedia and Digital Systems (ROMS) using a licence similar to those held by Russian radio stations. AllOfMP3 stated that this agreement allowed it to distribute music legally from all artists and all labels, but this was disputed by most record labels, who generally did not recognize ROMS or believe that it had the authority to distribute their works. The rub is that AllOfMP3 made no claim as to its legality outside of Russia, but because it was Internet based it was therefore accessible to the world, and in practice its location was not relevant.

The first response to this unforeseen clash of jurisdictions was political in the form of threatened sanctions, and in June 2006, *The New York Times* reported that US trade negotiators had warned Russia that the continued existence of AllOfMP3 would jeopardise Russia's entry into the World Trade Organisation. This was bolstered later that year by a lawsuit on behalf of EMI, Sony BMG, Universal Music Group, and Warner Music Group who claimed a total of 1.65 trillion USD in damages – a sum that exceeded Russia's entire GDP.

In August 2007, Denis Kvasov, head of the company that owned AllofMP3 was acquitted of all charges stemming from copyright infringement and in May 2008, the American music labels dropped their case against AllOfMP3, with enhanced payment procedures being introduced.

In the case of The Pirate Bay, when police finally raided their offices in 2008 and took their computer equipment, it became clear that this wasn't simply about people wanting music and films for free but that it was about people seeking change – and on 17 April 2009, Peter Sunde, Fredrik Neij, Gottfrid Svartholm and Carl Lundström became some of the world's best-known Internet rebels when in a blinding flash of judicial belligerence they were found guilty of assistance to copyright infringement and sentenced to one year in prison and payment of a fine of around £2.8 million. As with other corporate-led battles this prosecution wasn't a clean-cut affair with goodies on one side and baddies on the other, and hacked emails from an unknown source in September 2007 showed that the anti-piracy company Media-Defender had planned to employ programmers to damage The Pirate Bay's sites, and that the MPAA's member studios hired the company to pollute The Pirate Bay's torrent database ('I Was a Hacker for the MPAA', *Wired*, 22nd October 2007).

Then, post-trial it emerged that Judge Thomas Norström[9] in addition to ruling in other copyright cases,

9 'The best judge money can buy' (https://encyclopediadramatica.rs/The_Pirate_Bay) retrieved September 2017

also just happened to be a member of the Swedish Association for the Protection of Industrial Property and the Swedish Copyright Association (*The Independent,* 23rd April 2009)! These facts were largely brushed aside however, and before anyone could say 'conflict of interest big enough to drive a tank through' or indeed 'corgis of censorship' it was announced that these bias allegations were not to be investigated, as the judge in question announced that there was no tug of war between his various activities outwith his judicial role, and the case in question.

In spite of this The Pirate Bay persists and it does so by not being in any one fixed location. Now, The Pirate Bay is not based on a server in Sweden but uses a series of independent virtual computers and an infrastructure that allows it to be distributed over many different geographic positions – and thus, as Dramatica phrases it, 'The Pirate Bay's efforts of spreading Photoshop, movies, games and otherwise super expensive shit go largely unhindered.'

This may be a short-term victory for The Pirate Bay, but the real point is that current laws are not fit for purpose, essentially because they are always tied to legal jurisdictions. In bringing this to light, The Pirate Bay have done a great service to the Internet, whether they have been likeable or even criminal in doing so. In fact what they were found guilty of is as follows: 'Providing a conduit for others to break the law, rather than breaching copyright themselves'. This in turn is interesting, because plenty of more legitimate and corporate websites, including Google, Facebook and YouTube, also host or provide links to copyright material.

To return to basics, it may be helpful to trace the evolution of copyright in particular as it affects the producers of music. It is true that once upon a time the only way that musicians could make any money was by performing that music, and with the invention of recording technology, musicians felt that their paid work would dry up because with recordings available they would not be needed for public entertainment.

As it transpired, the recording industry offered new and magnificent opportunities for musicians because consumers instantly spent more time and money on music, and so everyone benefitted. With the advent of radio, similar discussions took place regarding the legality of a medium that played music for free and there was a fair amount of corporate hand-wringing at the prospect of people being able to listen to music in their homes without paying for it – but as it transpired, radio was the best thing that ever happened to the music industry, and even more markets were developed.

With the advent of the tape cassette the same process was repeated and with the arrival of the CD things were fine for a short period because these shiny new optical storage formats could not be copied or illegally disseminated. With the advent of the Internet however – which has no centralised controlling person or point – media began to be shared, and in huge quantities – and a proper panic has ensued in which the legislators will never be able to catch up with their foes, the pirates. This trend will not end here – indeed, have a think about what will happen when 3D printing takes off. I would foresee for example that when 3D printing technology is widely available, pirated spare parts and other consumer items will be accessible, so we will not need to purchase originals when we need something, such as a component for a machine, or a new pair of shoes.

The case of The Pirate Bay has hopefully shown that instead of going after single entities that facilitate file-sharing, we will one day have to hold a widespread public debate. Copyright in this context is not a stand-alone issue, and while activists continue to bring this to public attention, many companies and lobbyists are proposing controls over the Internet as a whole, with ruling measures such as the ACTA agreement coming into effect.

Controversies regarding intellectual property habitually arise when widespread user activity conflicts with the interests of lobbying groups. The largest of these lobbying groups is the IIPA (International Intellectual Property Alliance) a coalition of trade associations which include the Business Software Alliance and the Motion Picture Association of America. A common reaction among users interested in privacy, as well as those interested in piracy, has been an increased use in encryption technologies, such as VPNs (virtual private networks). These, as the name suggests, are virtual versions of secure physical networks, which users connect to and which offer the benefits of privacy and other resources that private networks have over the Internet as a whole. Privacy is increased with a VPN because the user's original IP address (and their probable identity and geographic location) is replaced with one from the VPN provider. Because a more widely anonymous Internet makes it harder for law enforcement to track down users who have downloaded pirated material, the emphasis therefore is still on companies that are providing links to the material, although it is a losing battle.

The fact that some of the arguments made by groups like the Pirate Party have entered the mainstream indicates a degree of success on their part, and perhaps the widespread practice of Internet piracy is something of a vote of no-confidence in the current set up, with its old-fashioned legislation. Repressive measures have not been successful, even though these are what lobbyists are still calling for – but the lobbyists will continue to lose the battles, even if in the meantime they enjoy the protection of the laws they have themselves helped bring to bear.

In 1994, law professor Paul Goldstein coined the term 'celestial jukebox' to refer to a vision of a networked database of consumable on-demand media – a lot like Spotify or Netflix in fact, which are both commercial music streaming and video services. On this model, everybody would pay for what they consumed and content producers would benefit from a massive shared central pot. This is to an extent successful, but thus far the industry has not properly discussed matters with copyright activists and software pirates, because in order to monetise and protect their copyright, their suggested controls will lead to the irreversible spoiling of the Internet. That's to say that for the transfer of music and video files to be managed so that every action is tracked, traced and monetised, we'd have to forego our relatively free Internet and opt for an Internet controlled by regulation and incorporation. Since 1994 there have been other developments, such as blockchain technology, which could offer even fairer models, and these will be discussed in the final chapter.

Arjen Kamphuis, ever the consummate hacktivist, has a lot to say on this, and for him it hangs together as one subject – cryptography. Copyright law, government IT policies and cryptocurrency are all at stake when it comes to maintaining a free Internet, he argues, and he takes part in what are called cryptoparties at which technology and security experts get together with people who are interested in learning more about privacy and security. Cryptoparties are a mixture of teaching and feedback for security experts and novices and one of the reasons they happen is that the basics of modern technology are ill-understood at best. In running cryptoparties across the world, hackers and activists have taken it upon themselves to rectify this by encouraging people to take Internet security into their own hands. 'Nobody gets paid for anything,' says Kamphuis, 'it's just something you do because you feel it's important.'

Even if there is a tension between what the Internet can achieve and what is legal, this is not going to stop people exploring the uses of these and associated technologies. Supposing for example that using the obvious benefits of the Internet you devised a service by which you could transfer large files quickly from place to place – and let's imagine that your idea involved an ad-supported video hosting service, an image hosting service, a video streaming service, and a place you could upload your entire music library.

This would probably be the most quintessential Internet-age service we could conceive of, but it would come with one large problem, which would be that in effecting these transfers, such a service would at any given time be hosting an uncountable quantity of copyrighted material. Having established that as the case, governments around the world would immediately assert that your website was being used for criminal purposes – and it must be assumed that if you are hosting material, then you must somehow be responsible for it, and if you seek to make profit from the material, then problems will arise.

This chain of events was what drove the prosecution and persecution of the German-born technologist Kim Dotcom. Dotcom – born Kim Schmitz in 1974 – was the founder of now-defunct file hosting service Megaupload, which offered a largescale file hosting service. Dotcom was subsequently accused by the US Department of Justice of copyright infringement and a host of other charges, such as money laundering, racketeering and wire fraud, and in January 2012, the New Zealand Police raided his home in Auckland and placed him in custody in response to the US charges. The audacious and movie-style raid on Kim Dotcom's home was sensational as it involved helicopters, dogs, and 76 officers, many armed with military-style weaponry. Dotcom was accused of costing the entertainment industry $500 million through unlicensed content uploaded to Megaupload which had 150 million registered users – and after years of legal battles, Dotcom is still fighting his extradition to the United States.

Kim Dotcom's service was there to make money, that much is true, but Megaupload was not a website that deliberately pirated material, even though piracy appears to be an obvious corollary of its operation. Kim Dotcom is not an Internet service provider and yet epic quantities of pirated material pass through the hands of ISPs every second of every day, and yet they are not asked to do anything about it as they are not hosting it. It is not entirely clear therefore why the US – with then Attorney General Eric Holder leading the charge – were going after Kim Dotcom. If they are using their prosecutorial capabilities to pursue a guy who is in effect a technology innovator, then there is something wrong. After all, one of the things that Kim Dotcom's services were offering was privacy. Who for example would upload anything to any Google, Microsoft or Apple server, knowing that the

US, UK, AU, NZ and CAN governments have access to it? Nobody.

As with Julian Assange, prosecutors in America seem obsessed with Kim Dotcom, and they appear keen to bully him and his Internet services into submissive oblivion. Kim Dotcom, however, is not an Internet pirate, and if anything he has been working to meet users' needs and avoid piracy. This may be exampled in MEGA, which is a cloud storage and file hosting service that Dotcom commenced in 2013. I use MEGA myself, and it is a great service, and far finer in many respects than Google Drive et al. The essential fact about MEGA is that it seeks to be a safe place for people to upload data – it is so safe in fact that MEGA itself will not know what you have placed on their servers. This works by encrypting the data first in your browser without you even knowing it, with the end goal being that your data is encrypted point to point, without MEGA or anyone else being able to see it. MEGA has now over 50 million registered users and more than 20 billion files have been uploaded to the service, and although nobody but their owners know what these files are, we can't simply assume that because they are private that they must somehow be bad.

Kim Dotcom's prosecution has been anything but smooth and authorities even decided to raid his mother's house in Germany, closing down the street she lived on and arriving with demands for items, including her car. Worse, the case against Kim Dotcom has a definite political aspect to it, and so it is not a simple criminal prosecution, even if that is how it appears. The influence of the MPAA (Motion Picture Association of America) is clear in these chain of events, with many news sources reporting that comments made by Chairman and CEO Chris Dodd implied that the MPAA would, for example, withdraw support for President Obama if something were not done (*The Independent*, 6th June 2013). In these and other reports, one can certainly detect the monopoly of the content conglomerates – and after all, it does seem strange that they would send two helicopters and over 70 police to arrest one unarmed man who is accused of copyright infringement. On top of this, Kim Dotcom's website was shut down immediately, which gave the impression that a judgment had already been made.

The attack on Kim Dotcom has all the hallmarks of a political hit, and more than a suggestion of prosecutorial overreach. In September 2012, it was revealed that the New Zealand Government Communications Security Bureau (GCSB), a member of the Five Eyes, had spied on Kim Dotcom, illegally helping police to locate him and monitor his communications in the weeks prior to the raid on his house. The GCSB are not of course allowed to spy on New Zealand citizens or permanent residents, a fact that led to an apology and admission of wrongdoing from Prime Minister John Key.

'I apologise to Mr Dotcom,' he said. 'I apologise to New Zealanders because every New Zealander is entitled to be protected from the law when it comes to the Government Communications Security Bureau, and we failed to provide that appropriate protection for him.'

'I apologise,' he might have said – however all of this after the fact does not demonstrate contrition but merely points to illegal acts on behalf of prosecutors whose interests are far from clear. The raid on Kim Dotcom's house was yet the most public and militarised salvo in the war on copyright infringement, and it looks increasingly like the actions of the Five Eyes partnership, whose agendas are cybercrime and signals intelligence, are now to include the protection of American business interests.

I wonder in fact if this is a future trend to be aware of? It used to be the case that the limits of our freedoms were controlled by the existence of nation states, although now perhaps terms of service documents from websites may act as a new kind of law that shapes our actions.

How can we decide who has the authority to make decisions about what is acceptable use of data, and how do we ensure these people do not abuse their power? The issue is not new or even specific to the Internet age but is a question for citizens and governments. As the only legitimate purpose of government is to serve citizens, we do not like to see states dealing out disproportionate punishments and conspiring against people's legitimate right to communicate – but having said that no government has tackled the heart of the issue, which should include the public renovation of copyright.

To get a handle on the many laws both passed and

proposed when it comes to copyright and similar protections can be time consuming, and as this book is published, a new set of data laws are being locked into place in the UK, some of them to allow people in the British Isles to send data to and from the EU.

Indeed, in May 2018, the GDPR, a new set of cross-EU data rules will come into force and the UK's data rules must therefore be updated to match them so they are equivalent to the EU's laws after Brexit occurs.

The new UK laws, which are summed up in what is called the Data Protection Bill (2017), cover the following basic facts of our modern lives:

- The right to be forgotten, under which consumers should be able to ask businesses and organisations for access to their personal data and for it to be wiped. This matches the current EU legislation, although in addition, the UK will legislate to require social media organisations to delete all of a person's material from before they were over 18, if they ask for it.
- Under the Data Protection Bill, the definition of personal data will be expanded to reflect our maddened times, meaning that IP addresses (used to identify a specific phone or computer), internet cookies (info about your web browsing habits) and DNA will be classed as 'personal data'[10].

10 The Data Protection Act of 1998 describes 'personal data' as data which relate to a living individual who can be identified (a) from those data, or (b) from those data

• As consent for website privacy policies is usually assumed and our addition to email and other lists is made on an opt-out basis, the new laws will make consent explicit; that is to say that when we are on the Internet we will have to opt in to being put on cold-calling and other lists so that we are more aware that their information is being passed on to marketing companies.

• Finally, as increasing amounts of services (including insurance claims and job applications) are relying on automation, and because we can all be profiled by algorithms using our personal data, we will in future, we are told, be able to have certain actions performed by a person, rather than a machine, if we so request it (*The Telegraph,* 7th August 2017).

The good news is that so far, the bill is broadly welcomed by the organisations who monitor such things, such as the openrightsgroup.org who commented: 'We welcome the government's intention to bring European data protection laws into UK law. It will strengthen everyone's ability to control what data can be collected about them and how it can be used' (Javier Ruiz, Director, Open Rights Group, 7th August 2017).

In recent decades however, there have been a bewildering array of ill-fitted foot-in-mouth laws that have almost entirely been conceived of in the USA, which

and other information which is in the possession of, or is likely to come into the possession of, the data controller.

have related to privacy, piracy and other aspects of Internet living.

Here are a few of the major acts and laws you may have heard of that have been in the news in recent years; you will recognise some of them, and even though you may continue to enjoy media, both legal or barely legal, there are certain principles apparent in their enumeration, as they indicate a state/corporate nexus grappling to keep control, keep profits and keep up.

Emmanuel Goldstein wrote of them in *2600*, Spring 2012: 'Only the names change; the game is always the same. Think of them as threats which never go away.'

CISA

The Cybersecurity Information Sharing Act is a US law that allows sharing of Internet traffic information between the government and companies. This act was introduced in 2015 and has been called the worst anti-privacy law since the US Patriot Act, as it gives businesses legal protections which encourage them to share data on 'hacking threats' with the government. This can be interpreted as saying that immunity is offered to corporations to give up data that they have collected under the legal fiction that the data is not that of the customers, but is the property of the corporations who collected it. According to Justin Amash, an American attorney and Republican member of Congress, the CISA act was negotiated in secret by a few members of Congress and was added quietly to a two-thousand-page omnibus bill, and that most representatives were probably at the time unaware that they even voted for it.

DMCA

Signed into law in 1998, the Digital Millennium Copyright Act criminalises the distribution of technology that could be used to circumvent copyright protection mechanisms and anything else that facilitates copyright infringement on the Internet. The Online Copyright Infringement Liability Limitation Act (OCILLA) is included in the DMCA and limits the liability of service providers for the actions of their users. The Electronic Frontier Foundation (eff.org) has fought against the DMCA provisions in the courts, Congress and other forums, and continues to work hard to make sure that DMCA 'safe harbours', which protect service providers from monetary liability based on the allegedly infringing activities of third parties, continue to shelter innovation and creativity. 'In practice, the DMCA anti-circumvention provisions have done little to stop Internet piracy,' argue the EFF. 'Yet the DMCA has become a serious threat that jeopardizes fair use, impedes competition and innovation, and chills free expression and scientific research.'

SOPA

The Stop Online Piracy Act was a bill tabled in the American House in 2012 which offered the US Justice Department and copyright holders the power to take down websites due to alleged copyright infringement without hearing a defence by the website owners. Incredibly, this Act permitted powerful copyright holders to have a whole website taken down and not solely the pages that contained the infringing material – and this was without anyone even entering a courtroom. On 18th January 2012, the English pages of Wikipedia shut down for 24 hours to protest this draconian legal move, and after worldwide protest which saw many Internet users turn to activism for the very first time, a petition with over 14 million names was presented to the American Congress and the bill was withdrawn – demonstrating that even if your vote doesn't count, your dissent certainly can. By chance, the 2014 Sony Pictures hack showed that the MPAA has continued to consider and argue for SOPA-like powers since the bill died. The hacked Sony emails showed that the MPAA was exploring new methods to implement similar regulations, such as using the All Writs Act to 'allow [the MPAA] to obtain court orders requiring site blocking without first having to sue and prove the target ISPs are liable for copyright infringement' (*The Verge*, 12th December 2014).

CISPA

After SOPA failed, ever-appetent American legislators introduced the Cyber Intelligence Sharing and Protection Act (CISPA). The purpose of the CISPA bill was to defend against cyber-threats by allowing the military and government agencies we have already discussed to

PETER BURNETT

collect and share private data from companies without a warrant. The potentially damaging thing about this bill is that it gave the American government permission to monitor nearly all Internet activity – even the 95% of the planet that are not American – and to use that information without liability. One ramification is that if a government or military agency shares your information because they deem you a threat and it turns out to be a mistake, you will not be able to establish a legal recourse. Although it was first passed in 2011, CISPA isn't quite there yet – a fact made worse by a scandal in December 2015, when CISA, which is a version of the CISPA bill, was hidden in the federal budget bill. The purpose for placing CISA within this omnibus bill was that it further reduced the possibility of debate over its surveillance-friendly provisions, a fact which outraged activists and avoided the mass public objections that had blocked previous bills. If you run a check on the American companies that back this bill however, you'll find all our favourites in there – from Facebook to Microsoft and all major communication companies between.

ACTA

The Anti-Counterfeiting Trade Agreement is a multinational bill that was signed in Tokyo in 2011 and was established to help prevent copyrighted ideas and material being stolen via any medium, including the Internet. The side effect of this act is that it obliges ISPs (Internet service providers) to police content, and although the bill

140

has been ratified by many countries, it is unclear what powers it affords whom. What is clear is that ACTA is one of many baffling attempts to control copyright at the very highest level, although activists such as those at the EFF (Electronic Frontier Foundation) who analyse these legal processes – most of which are entirely secret – suspect that these bills are pressing us towards a regime for global Internet regulation. It is possible that behind ACTA is a desire to burden the whole world with US-style rules that require ISPs to remove material that is accused of infringing copyright without evidence or trial – but this has already proved problematic, because this provision allows entire websites to be censored, even if they are just accused of copyright infringement.

SESTA

Once upon a time on the Internet, you could say what you liked! In fact, barring hate-speech and other incendiary and illegal forms of communication, you still can, and you can do so knowing that you are 100% responsible for it all. SESTA (which stands for Stop Enabling Sex Traffickers Act) has an important purpose, but it goes about its work by imposing criminal liability on message boards and any other type of website where people can comment or upload material. What SESTA proposes to do is shift liability for trafficking offenses (which are already illegal) to online platforms, and it requires that these platforms be responsible for their users' speech. Under current US law, companies and people that provide online platforms for others to share speech and content cannot be held responsible for the speech of others, but SESTA proposes to shift that balance. Of course, such legislation is more of a threat to start-ups, small blogs and anyone else that doesn't have the money to fight litigation, but in principle it is probably wrong to shift this onus to website providers, who may have thriving comments sections and other public facilities. This protection of intermediaries is in fact currently guaranteed under the Communications Decency Act of 1996, in Section 230, and it's been 230 that has allowed the social media industry to bloom to such a massive extent, and it has even allowed Wikipedia and similar sites to grow. It appears that pro-censorship groups have been trying to have Section 230 gutted for some time now, however, and it has been argued that with SESTA these same lobbyists are trying to do so once again by rallying around something revolting in the form of sex trafficking. I'd like to quote Elliot Harmon, of the Electronic Frontier Foundation:

> This is exactly why we have to speak up and tell Congress that this is the wrong solution. Once every few years, geeks have to get together to explain to lawmakers how the Internet works.
> (*2600*, Autumn 2017)

PIPA

The PROTECT IP Act (standing for Preventing Real Online Threats to Economic Creativity and Theft of

Intellectual Property Act) is an acronym within an acronym, referring to a proposed bill that would have a significant effect on free speech. One of the act's goals was to de-list objectionable websites, which would have been available to the rest of the world, but which would have appeared not to exist at all in the US. Google chairman Eric Schmidt was one of several high-profile figures who vowed that the act would be unfair and that his company would fight it. In the UK and the USA such measures have been proposed several times and are thought of as a good way of filtering out file-sharing and torrent sites, which could be then be banned. The argument goes that since the act was not intended to focus solely on foreign sites and would extend to domestic websites that facilitated or somehow enabled infringement, protected speech on legitimate sites such as YouTube, Twitter, and Facebook would also be targeted.

★

As it happens, and in consideration of this last legal act, some of this de-listing is done anyway by HR departments or so-called 'Trust and Safety Councils' at these large firms, which are beginning to use their own private power to shut down or demonetise channels they do not like. Often this is in response to advertisers, but sometimes it is political censorship. You may imagine that these take-downs and attacks are based on hate-speech, racism and other unacceptable behaviour, but the 2017 case of the University of Toronto's Professor Jordan Peterson, who was refused access to his Google services, is an interesting example, as Peterson is a respectable educator, who exhibits none of these tendencies. One can make a guess as to why Professor Peterson lost access to his Gmail service and his YouTube channel, but Google offered no explanation.

> It seems to me that the ability to post video lectures online, with the ability to reach hundreds of thousands or even millions of people (and for that to happen in a more or less permanent form) is a revolution equivalent to the Gutenberg press, says Professor Peterson. I now have had more than six million views on my YouTube channel. That's incomparably more people than have bought my book or read my papers. So maybe that's the real future of education – particularly given what the universities have done with the social sciences and humanities. Why not educate everyone?
>
> (Professor Jordan Peterson, *Washington Times*, 1st August 2017)

The professor came to worldwide prominence in 2016 for opposition to Canada's C-16 bill, which would have required him as a public servant to use genderless pronouns. Although no reason was given for the Google ban, which included him being refused access to his email account, it remains a chilling thought that this can happen, especially when we consider that Google, Twitter, YouTube and similar platforms are virtually public services to us.

If the proliferation of these legal bills proves anything, then, it is an overbearing fear of Internet technology shown by those who cannot see far beyond the commercial benefits. ACTA has been devised alongside the comprehensive Economic and Trade Agreement (CETA) – the Agreement on Trade-Related Aspects of Intellectual Property Rights (TRIPS) – and the EU Enforcement Directive (IPRED). To these we may add a proposed Protection of Broadcasts and Broadcasting Organizations Treaty – and the EU Telecoms Package – neither of which have a fearful acronymic handle, and so may yet prove to be immune to citizen activism.

Some say that the solution to issues of piracy, privacy and free speech is stronger intellectual property laws and that these be coupled with technological advances, while others argue that piracy is inevitable, as it always has been with or without the Internet.

Nothing can in fact be predicted – and when Danish Internet service providers banned traffic from The Pirate Bay in 2008 the overall global effect was a marginal increase of about 3% in Internet piracy, possibly because the publicity made people aware that such services existed in the first place.

Although Steve Jobs is quoted as arguing 'it is piracy, not overt online music stores, which is our main competitor,' piracy is not a market competitor but a consequence of technology, combined with unfair legislation.

Kim Dotcom has argued the opposite of Steve Jobs' position, stating that: 'It's the big boys, the Googles of this world that are already benefiting from piracy and not paying the artists a dime.'

A certain clarity may be available in the truly levelling nature of the Internet itself which empowers creators of all ages, experience and genres to generate, market and distribute material without any corporate backing – although as Kim Dotcom's quotation suggests, there remains a point at which artists are going to be in thrall to some conglomerate or other, so long as corporate and government interests control the network.

There are several pertinent threats to the Internet which come under the above heading of 'government and corporate interest controlling the network', and from time to time you may hear the debate concerning one of them – net neutrality.

To describe what the phrase 'net neutrality' implies, you might imagine yourself in the near future opening your web browser to find that you can't get the Internet you want, at the speed you think appropriate. This could be happening because your Internet service provider (ISP), as your gatekeeper to the Internet has decided which sites and services you can visit.

Much is possible. Under such conditions your email service, choice of social media and even your web browser could be determined by your ISP, who may also have introduced a tiered pricing system based on how much you are willing to pay each month. It would be like your current cable and satellite television services, insofar as the more you pay, the more channels you would have, and faster.

The concept of net neutrality however predates the Internet by over a century and when the idea was first put forward in the age of the telegraph, it was decided that regardless of where telegraphs or later telephone calls were going to and from, or what their contents were, they would be delivered impartially and in the order they were received.

If a pay-for-service Internet were permitted, and if ISPs began to follow free-market dictates, then free, private, independent and personal websites could likely suffer, as they would not be able to afford the fees required of an ISP, and would be served more slowly – if at all.

There has been a long debate about whether net neutrality should be required by law in the United States, and its advocates have raised concerns about the ability of broadband providers to use what is known as their 'last mile' infrastructure to block Internet applications and content, and even to block out competitors (*Cyberspace's Architectural Constitution*, Lawrence Lessig, June 2000).

In the meantime, it's another battlefront in the war and although attempts to impose various kinds of traffic throttling have been made by Internet service providers, activists and politicians continue to campaign against this notion, potentially in fear of huge Internet content providers (or potentially just one!) that want to set up their own networks.

As much as it sounds like a bad idea, what's been lost in the shuffle is that with net neutrality removed, there would be a limit to where you could go on the Internet. Perhaps the end result will be that given the choice between being able to go where you want a little slower or go to a few places quickly, most people are going to go with full access.

CHAPTER 5 THE VALUED PRESS

Glenn Greenwald, Barrett Brown and the Mossack Fonesca Papers

> This is the world we accept if we continue to avert our eyes, and it promises to get much worse.
> Barrett Brown

Why do governments wish to pry so actively into the lives of citizens? Even to research this question takes a fearless kind of journalist, one prepared to swim against the prevailing stream of popular media that has a tendency to mislead, as it has done in the case of Edward Snowden.

In his book *No Place to Hide - Edward Snowden, the NSA, and the Surveillance State* freelancer Glenn Greenwald recalls how, in the wake of the Snowden revelations that he helped publish, there was a consensus that Edward Snowden was a Chinese spy. After two weeks, Greenwald tells us, when Edward Snowden travelled to Russia in an effort to find a route to Ecuador, these same reports switched to speculating on the possibility that Snowden was a Russian spy in the pay of Vladimir Putin. In the UK, these and similar allegations were reported by both *The Daily Mail* and *The Mirror*, and in the US, *The Wall Street Journal* carried stories echoing these claims, even suggesting that Russia and China were working together on a conspiracy to undermine United States security. The other aspect that Greenwald highlights was a co-ordinated media effort to portray Edward Snowden – within 48 hours of anyone ever having heard of him – as 'a fame-seeking narcissist' – a phrase that appeared repeatedly at the time, pointing to a supposed mental imbalance in the mind of the whistle-blower.

These reports, which often included the precise and by this time oft-repeated phrase 'fame-seeking narcissist' were reiterated from Fox News to *The New Yorker* and echoed the treatment of previous whistle-blowers like Daniel Ellsberg, who was recurrently smeared by the Nixon administration. Similar attempts have been made to overlay the reputations of Julian Assange and Chelsea Manning, both of whom helped deliver material that made many political administrations uncomfortable. This is a straightforward way of excluding these individuals by discrediting them in the eyes of the public and effectively stigmatising everything they say and do.

A further attached cliché is the assertion that Snowden's releases have helped terrorists and other enemies of America, and that innocent people will lose their lives because of his leak. Aside from the fact that this claim is repeated without any suggestion that any evidence will be presented, it is a familiar trope and is very much to be expected when someone makes themselves an enemy of such a powerful administration as the US represents.

Lessons from the past then, meant that when Edward Snowden approached the media through selected journalists he did so with an understanding of how he wished the data to be reported. Credit in particular goes to the journalist Glenn Greenwald and the filmmaker Laura Poitras who reported on the Snowden disclosures. Both Greenwald and Poitras had been working on surveillance issues for some time and understood that the public treated the issue of privacy as remote and abstract, and so the overall effect of Snowden's work has been a success insofar as interest in the topic is sustained years later. This was a strategy on the part of Snowden and his journalists and not a fortunate by-product of the reckless and indiscriminate leak we may have been led to believe it was.

It is a customary element of our discourse that governments will tell their citizens that the state is committed to security, although this assertion does not ask who the enemies of any given state are. This is because, as it turns out, one of the prime enemies is *you*! Every power system believes this, and this is one of the reasons why they need to know everything about you that they can.

Further, it appears that genuine security is almost never the reason for secrecy, but because power must work unseen, secrecy is *de facto* required.

On this subject, Edward Snowden has been obliged to speculate on some of the very basics of what a free society might look like:

Going to war with people that are not our enemy in places that are not a threat doesn't make us safe. And that applies if it's in Iraq or on the Internet. The Internet is not the enemy. The economy is not the enemy. American businesses, Chinese businesses and any other company out there is a part of our society, it's a part of our interconnected world. There are ties of fraternity that bond us together. If we destroy these bonds by undermining the standards of security and the manner of behaviour that nations and citizens around the world expect us to abide by.

It is now not an unusual idea that the broadcast media constricts the range of accepted political discourse, and this realisation occurred thanks in part to the Internet, which has allowed people to share and experience a wider perspective, and in turn this has led to a deeper and more widespread analysis of major media. At the same time the Internet has broadened the scope of what journalism can be.

The UK's most popular news websites are still operated by large corporations however, topped by the BBC, *The Telegraph*, *The Mail Online* and *The Guardian*. There are no blogs in the entire top 40 of the UK's news websites, and nor are there likely to be in the near future. This doesn't affect the popularity of what may be called citizen journalism, which could be loosely described as bloggers, sometimes untrained as journalists, collecting, reporting, analysing, and disseminating news and information. The advantages of citizens acting as journalists is that they are not constrained by the needs of larger news outlets, who are just as answerable to advertisers as they are intimate with the economic and political powers they should be watchdogging. Ironically, cuts in newspaper staff have prompted mergers in the news industry which may be further limiting the range of viewpoints that have access to mass media, and with media outlets owned by for-profit conglomerates and supported by corporate advertisers, independent journalism is compromised even further.

Internet technologies have changed the way we interact with all media, although for events occurring live, I think most of us would still turn to the old-fashioned television. One striking exception to this occurred during the 2012 arrest of journalist and activist Barrett Brown, an event which was captured live on a video chatroom supported by Tinychat. There hasn't in fact been anything quite like Barrett Brown's arrest in the history of the Internet and while activists have been pursued, entrapped and arrested, it's usually happened in secret and never in an unplanned live feed.

Although Barrett Brown had been on a collision course with the law for several months, the aggression with which law enforcement prosecuted him was a shock for all who were following his work. The lessons acted out in this case show the lengths the US in particular is prepared to go to in its efforts to gag any person who concerns themselves with certain aspects of their business.

Barrett Brown's interest as a journalist is the public and private relationships that comprise the cyber military-industrial complex. Before his arrest, Brown was delving into deals and routine practises which were carried out between America's private security contractors and the government agencies to which they sold their services – and this brings us back to our old friends at Stratfor. While it may not be ethical or even legal for governments to spy on their citizens and gather intelligence using false social media accounts, Internet trolling and misinformation, these techniques are employed by private individuals and firms who consequently sell their information to the authorities. The development and employment of spy software is a massive business, and while the data that is sold by private firms may not be actionable in a court, it is still of use to state services.

This is something that is still barely reported upon because even though governments are expected to be transparent in their operations, private firms are not. This was the spur which set Barrett Brown's reportage into gear and as his work took off. The work not only took off but it paid off, and soon into his research, Barret Brown found that news outlets were interested, and he published articles on this subject for *The Guardian*'s Comment is Free pages, *The Huffington Post* and other journals, blogs and outlets.

As a web-based nucleus for this work, Barrett Brown established a public wiki that aimed to gather information on private security firms, and material for this database (called Project PM) was donated by other activists and journalists. Naturally enough, this wiki was not liked by the intelligence contracting industry, and in 2011, leading up to Barrett Brown's arrest, netizens[11], journalists and other interested parties were treated to a strange parade of attacks on Brown from not only contractors posing as Internet trolls, but from others that leaped in to become a part of what seemed like an amusing controversy.

Controversy turned to action on the part of the government when on 6th March 2012, the FBI executed search warrants at Brown's apartment and his mother's house seeking evidence of alleged crimes. What the FBI were looking for, but did not find, were hacked records relating to the security contractors HBGary, Infragard and Endgame Systems – and as they are wont to do in such situations, agents took possession of the journalist's computers, along with anything else they could find which seemed relevant, including video games and other CDs. The assumption was that if Barrett Brown were in control of the wiki Project PM, then he must have access to any stolen data that was posted on it by others, or have even stolen the data himself – but none of this was true and could not be proven to be true, and so by September,

---

11 Netizen: Any person with an online presence who wishes to be declared a member of the greater society that is cyberspace. (Definition by Daelphinux, *2600*, Summer 2017).

Barrett Brown, still without his computers, reached the end of his patience and uploaded three videos to You-Tube in which he attacked the FBI for their handling of the affair. In the September 2012 videos Barrett Brown identified key figures in his harassment, and issued an ultimatum demanding the return of his computers. As can be seen in these videos – which are still on YouTube – Barrett Brown talks of how he and his mother were at the time being harassed. Brown also asserted that a dirty tricks campaign was being played against him, either by the FBI or its contractors, and the dirty tricks that he cited included the public release of private information concerning him, a technique called 'doxing'. In his uploads to YouTube, Barrett Brown then stated that if he did not have his computers returned, he would visit this same tactic against the FBI's arresting officer, Special Agent Robert Smith.

Most of us would be able to assert – even without the benefit of the practical example that Barrett Brown underwent – that threatening law enforcement officials in Texas is never going to end happily. And although the video uploads made by Barrett Brown were in effect an invitation to persecution, the subsequent detention and trial of the journalist only proved in the opinion of many that this was the sole actionable crime in this case – the charges being the threats against a federal law enforcement officer.

The final video that Barrett Brown uploaded before he was arrested is in its own way a masterpiece of tragedy, comedy, conspiracy and reportage. In the fifteen-minute film, in which Brown is seen in the throes of drug withdrawal, the journalist explains his determination to come off drugs, no matter what the emotional cost, and he discusses how the FBI has threatened his mother with obstruction of justice charges – a charge that was reduced to obstructing the execution of a search warrant in November 2013. Manic and eloquent by turns, Barrett Brown explains how private intelligence contractors have come to influence political power, and he demonstrates with specific examples how that power has been used against not just himself, but against foreign and domestic populations.

These assertions meant that the next day viewers of Tinychat were treated to one of the most stunning sights the Internet has ever beheld – the violent arrest of a journalist, live on air.

Brutal may be a judgemental description of that evening's arrest, but it is fair. Barrett Brown can be seen in clips of the arrest larking around on his webcam until with no warning we hear law enforcement officers break down his door. It's reported that for this unarmed journalist, eleven armed men were required, and rather than serving him with an arrest warrant, the FBI decided that anti-terrorist style tactics were required. We can only speculate on the effect this had, but we can be certain that any journalist at that time who was working on similar material must have been scared for their own situation. Days later, Brown managed to release a statement from jail describing how he was denied medical treatment for injuries inflicted upon him by the arresting team, as well as other medication necessary for his withdrawal.

Barrett Brown's indictment on 3rd October 2012 began an achingly long legal process that saw Brown remaining in jail for over two years – without bail – before he was even put on trial. The first indictment in the strange case of Barrett Brown was a portmanteau attempt to portray the otherwise peaceful writer as a threat to public safety by painstakingly looking at his Twitter timeline and assembling dozens of posts which by themselves did not amount to much, but when collected were intended to form the foundation of a prosecution. Despite messages such as this from Brown: 'Threat to put my mom in prison last mistake #AgentRobertSmith will ever fucking make', there was nothing within Brown's Twitter or on his blog that could lead to a successful prosecution, and so these charges were dropped and were followed in December 2012 with the accusation that Brown had 'trafficked in stolen authentication features' – meaning that he had for whatever purpose passed credit card data from one place to another. It was also alleged at this time that Barrett Brown possessed stolen credit card numbers and that this amounted to charges of Aggravated Identity Theft – assertions topped off by a charge the following year that Brown had tried to conceal evidence by hiding his laptops.

To rewind this case, it's clear that the madness of Barrett Brown's arrest was the culmination of a cat and mouse game between the hacker collective Anonymous and security consultants HBGary. Those who know anything about Anonymous will be aware that while certain individuals identifying with that group participate in socially-minded activism, a large amount are there for the lulz – basically a term referring to humorous Internet content, often involving the humiliation of others. In this case the lulz had been squarely directed at the misguided efforts of the CEO of HBGary, Aaron Barr, who announced in 2010 that he could identify key active members of Anonymous by using social media, social engineering, and by infiltration using false social media accounts. Along with this defiant announcement, the HBGary CEO proclaimed that he wanted to sell this data to the highest bidder and in the process reveal to the world the 'leaders' of Anonymous.

Aaron Barr's plan however turned out to be extremely unsophisticated, and had been dreamed up in December 2010, when sensational reports appeared that a large and mysterious group of hacktivists had been attacking the websites of MasterCard, PayPal, and Visa in retaliation for their having cut funding to WikiLeaks. Intrigued by this, Aaron Barr set up false Facebook accounts and friended Anonymous sympathisers, joined Anonymous chatrooms, and then tried to identify personalities by collating the times that relative users were appearing and disappearing from each website.

When Aaron Barr told the press that he was offering this information to the FBI among others, some members of Anonymous investigated for themselves and it was not long until Barr's claims were proved wrong when hackers compromised his email and found his data to be spurious at best, and completely wrong elsewhere. When emails stolen from HBGary were made public, it appeared that Barr had identified many innocent parties, Barrett Brown included, as infringing Anonymous activists. Immediately following this, members of the #Anonymous splinter group LulzSec took over Aaron Barr's Twitter account, his iPad (they claimed) and other accounts – all of which was easy as Barr had used the same relatively weak password ('kibafo33') for everything. It was this account hacking that incidentally introduced us to the turncoat FBI tipster Sabu, whom we heard about earlier.

The 68,000 emails that emerged as a result of this hack had been made publicly available as a torrent on The Pirate Bay but had only at this stage been briefly scanned, and there was still much to discover within them, including a dirty-tricks campaign against trade unions and WikiLeaks that Aaron Barr had been proposing. Many innocent parties aside from Barrett Brown were in the due course of time angered to see that they were being identified as criminals and 'leaders' of Anonymous by the improvident guesswork employed by Barr – and although the weekend of Barr's humiliation had been dramatic for HBGary, the fallout was to continue.

While the hackers responsible for the theft of the emails moved on to other projects – or in some cases, capture and detention – Barrett Brown's journalistic interest meant that he was willing to access stolen emails for information regarding the practices of HBGary and other security firms. It was subsequently shown that these other security firms including Palantir Technologies, Berico Technologies, and the law firm Hunton & Williams were cooperating on a project to discredit WikiLeaks. Other emails appeared to show the US Chamber of Commerce had contracted similar firms to discredit trade unions and liberal groups, while further investigation revealed the development of malicious spyware that had been designed to enable access to private and corporate computers that would not otherwise be allowed.

This was of interest to Barrett Brown as he was already gathering as much available material as possible on the workings of the burgeoning security industry that was providing the US administration with many of its spying services. This included Booz Allen Hamilton, the company that Edward Snowden worked for, but there are many such companies – often staffed by ex-CIA and government employees – and all bidding to sell their services to the state.

The issues for Barrett Brown were many, and not simply the ethics of such practices. Brown had already presented ground-breaking articles on software which could create an army of multiple fake social media profiles, and he had reported on Windows themes for video games and software proposed by HBGary, which would be used in the Middle East and Asian markets, and which would contain secret back-doors that only selected American companies would be able to access.

Despite being stopped in its tracks by the arrest of its founder, Project PM embodies some sound journalistic principles, which are perfectly complementary to the work of the whistle-blowers we have already read about. It was Brown's aim that Project PM be established to gather a critical mass of work from dependable bloggers and that the traditional media – used to reprinting or parroting government press statements and calling it 'news' – would be prompted to address issues in their own methods. A further aim of Project PM was to develop a resource which could provide bloggers and reporters with the best possible feed of raw information by which to produce content regarding security issues.

Before his arrest, Barrett Brown had already been making headway as he built Project PM, and in June 2011, he released an exclusive report about a surveillance contract called Romas/COIN which was discovered in e-mails hacked from HBGary. This research, which was subsequently reported in *The Guardian*, described new data-mining software which compromised mobile phones in Arab countries, and which was being operated by US military contractors such as – he suspected – Northrop Grumman and another large federal contractor TASC Software. Barrett Brown's report begins:

> For at least two years, the US has been conducting a secretive and immensely sophisticated

campaign of mass surveillance and data mining against the Arab world, allowing the intelligence community to monitor the habits, conversations, and activity of millions of individuals at once. And with an upgrade scheduled for later this year, the top contender to win the federal contract and thus take over the program is a team of about a dozen companies which were brought together in large part by Aaron Barr – the same disgraced CEO who resigned from his own firm earlier this year after he was discovered to have planned a full-scale information war against political activists at the behest of corporate clients.

Project PM, as instituted by Barrett Brown, was something new insofar as it co-ordinated whistle-blowing, hacking and journalism. Not all of the information on Project PM is secret, but much of it is still hard to access and is not yet of significant public interest. The question therefore regards a large overlap between government and private security, and it was for exploring this unlighted nexus of interests that Barrett Brown was imprisoned, and it is for these reasons that many considered him to be a political prisoner of the United States.

Journalist Joshua Kopstein (Al Jazeera, 15th February 2015) believes that the government considered Barrett Brown to be a threat and he suggests that its witnesses may have lied to secure this journalist's conviction. Further – as in the case of Edward Snowden and other whistle-blowers – the ongoing arguments have never been about the material that has been released, but about the status of the reporter. Much of Barrett Brown's 2014 trial was spent discussing the nature of Project PM – and it was even named as a criminal organisation – and if you had a log in to that wiki, as I did for example, these details were passed to the security services. Added to this was the same old argument concerning Barrett Brown's status as a journalist or not – a nonsensical debate that Glenn Greenwald has also been stuck with.

The public, however, like a judge and jury, should not be interested in extended discussion on whether a certain person is or is not a journalist and on the other hand, should very much like to hear about conspiring relations between security contractors and governments. That said, in February 2016, Barrett Brown received a National Magazine Award for political and social commentary, which probably demonstrates that he is a journalist – and although some would rather discuss his own faults, the real question is of course the validity of spending billions of dollars on spying on the public.

As Barrett Brown's eventual trial showed, many of the charges against him had no substance, but were an embarrassing attempt for the United States to pin what they had on a man they had kept in custody with no bail for several years already. The trafficking charge – most corrupt and false of all – was based on the fact that Brown had shared a link to stolen material hacked by activist Jeremy Hammond. Simply by sharing a link, the prosecution argued that Brown had been trafficking in anything that that link led to – in this case the stolen credit card details. But of course, as a journalist, Barrett Brown was not even aware of the credit card details and was in no way attempting to profit from them, but was merely placing the link in the chatroom over which he presided.

The subsequent storm regarding the shared link – 'From Link To Clink' – and the suggested 105 years which Brown was set to face for this act, drew comment from rights activists including Noam Chomsky, member of the Icelandic parliament Birgitta Jónsdóttir, and artist Shepard Fairey.

It is possible that the United States felt it could safely persecute Barrett Brown as he was a maverick and an unknown, and although the administration with its covey of judges, special agents and corporate security dealers has to a degree succeeded, the prosecution have at the same time brought about a greater awareness of Brown's work, and the work of those like him. Having been provoked by the federal authorities, Brown retaliated, and despite neither having carried out a single hack nor stolen any information, but only used Stratfor emails to point out wrongdoing in and around that company, Barrett Brown has been also required to pay damages to the company. He writes:

> I will spend the rest of my life in a strange state of post-cyberpunk indentured servitude to an

amoral private intelligence firm that's perhaps best known for having spied on Bhopal activists on behalf of Dow Chemical. That the prosecution did not quite manage to articulate how I did any damage to this particular company did not seem to dissuade [the trial Judge] in this matter.

The emails in the cache that Barrett Brown was using have at the same time revealed an obsession that government and related agencies have with spying on the public. The primary concern in Brown's case was that if he were to be convicted of sharing a link, other journalists and bloggers would be dissuaded from doing so. When this charge was abandoned in March 2014, a sound precedent was set insofar as citizens could continue to link to freely available information as part of journalistic investigation, and not be prosecuted for it.

Barrett Brown was released from prison on November 29th, 2016 and moved into a halfway house with five drug dealers close to downtown Dallas, Texas, from where he issued the message: 'Special thanks to Julian Assange and Sarah Harrison for releasing the 60,000 HB-Gary emails in honor of my release.' (*D. Magazine*, 1st December 2016)

The legal arguments concerning who is a journalist and who is not a journalist bloomed into a more mainstream melee in 2016 and 2017, in the form of the obsession with 'fake news'. The term 'fake news' isn't quite as clear cut as we might imagine, and does not strictly refer to stories that are made up in order to either fool the public or gain revenue in the form of advertising clicks. The more sinister implications of the concept of 'fake news' is that it somehow refers to journalists and news organisations that are in various manners of speaking 'off message' or do not wear the team colours of the mainstream. In part this means that the boom in citizen journalism can be tainted by association with this term, which has also been variously applied to conservative radio and Internet hosts, no matter how many millions of subscribers and followers they have. The problems that large media outlets like the BBC, CNN and Fox have always had, is that they carry not only advertorial content, but are susceptible to political spin and influence. This seems clearer than ever in the twenty-first century which features an Internet that allows citizens to stream live events and report on these with ease. These same news corporations are permanently as open to the accusation of their peddling not just fake but intentionally misleading news, just as readily as bloggers and YouTubers can be accused of circulating nonsense and lies. The worry for ourselves as consumers is that Facebook, Google and others are now reasonably far into the process of filtering our content, appointing themselves as arbiters of truth and objectivity, when in fact the idealists among us may wish to be able to contrast opinions from all news sites, regardless of their political leaning.

That Barrett Brown is a journalist is no longer widely questioned, and Brown's award for journalism was given to him for writing about solitary confine-ment, while he was himself in solitary within a Texas jail (American Society of Magazine Editors, 3rd February 2016).

Even the prosecutors in Barrett Brown's case knew that when Brown pasted the link to the Stratfor cache in his chatroom he had no intention of doing so to defraud card holders. What they did know was that Brown's Project PM team had been routinely scouring troves of both leaked and public documents to illuminate the threads connecting US spy bureaus, private intelli-gence firms (like Stratfor) and programs like TrapWire, which is a network of surveillance cameras which inter-act with a predictive software system designed to find patterns indicative of criminality. This information, as re-vealed by Barrett Brown, was being shared among banks, venture capitalists and intelligence contractors and with no sense of public accountability, and in Brown's opin-ion, this was a story worth pursuing.

The reasons why any of this is important be-comes clear when you consider how much the FBI was reliant upon data supplied by the intelligence contractor Aaron Barr. Barr's data, however, was wrong and not only identified Barrett Brown as a leader in Anonymous, but it mistakenly conflated him with three other people, including a professional gardener. That this information was then used by the FBI to activate a prosecution is bad enough. What is worse is that there was no check on this process, so once this ineptly gathered and false 'intelligence' had been delivered, the state leapt into action in an effort to find a crime that they could legally prosecute. Aside from the crime of threatening a law enforcement official, it took the agency a year to come up with the alleged crime of link-sharing – something that was unable to stick.

The only outstanding charge that makes any sense in the case of Barrett Brown, then, is the charge of threatening an FBI agent – a charge that only came about as a result of the agency harassing Brown in the first place. The companies and agencies in question may have not liked what Barrett Brown was doing but when it came to the crunch they ended up using guesswork to target him and then tried to force prosecutions for things that never happened – sometimes even including things that weren't even criminal – such as the sharing of hyperlinks.

The disgrace is on the US Department of Justice here, but with one journalist having been imprisoned through misadventure and having remained in various Texas jails for 63 months, it seems that the message is clear. If you explore the grey continent of deals that makes up the overlap between our governments and the private intelligence business – you may well regret it.

As the pendulum swings we can just as readily find the media co-operating with state or corporate authority, as elements of it did in the case of the Panama Papers leak of March 2016. These 11.5 million documents detailed financial and attorney-client information for more than 200,000 offshore entities, and were created by the law firm and corporate service provider Mossack Fonseca. What is curious about the Mossack Fonseca Papers (the Panamanian government strongly objects to the term 'The Panama Papers') is that first of all the leaks were not made public, but remained in the hands of selected journalists.

Aside from the creation of another compounded neologism in the form of the word *leaktivism*[12] the Mossack Fonseca Papers threw up further uncomfortable questions. It is curious for example that the leaks do not cover any significant US figures guilty of any of the fraud or tax evasion uncovered in this process. This strange state of affairs starts to make sense when you consider that the biggest corporate tax havens in the world are now in the US, in states like Nevada, Wyoming and South Dakota, all of which are emerging as the leading tax and secrecy havens for rich foreigners.

Could it be the case that the Mossack Fonseca leak was geared to tacitly promote the United States as the world's leading tax haven?[13] Not that there is any evidence of this, but suspicions remain, especially considering the selective nature of the content leaked. In one respect at least the public have been duped, because the

12 *Leaktivism* is a term used by leading Occupy Wall Street protestor Micah White, who is also known for coining the term *clicktivism*.
13 As reported in the article 'The World's Favorite New Tax Haven Is the United States' (Bloomberg, 27th January 2016) a managing director at Rothschild & Co. gave a public talk on how the world's wealthy elite can now avoid paying taxes by using American tax havens. 'His message was clear,' read the piece. 'You can help your clients move their fortunes to the United States, free of taxes and hidden from their governments. Some are calling it the new Switzerland.'

Mossack Fonseca Papers do not constitute a transparent leak in the same way that Edward Snowden's work or any WikiLeaks release did. If this is the case, then someone has turned the tables and what was described as the biggest document leak in history may in fact be a public relations exercise – and even if this is not true, that is what it is being used for.

Some overall data concerning the Mossack Fonseca Papers has been made available on a website run by the ICIJ at panamapapers.icij.org along with a list of the ICIJ journalists who spent a year analysing and reporting on the trove. Reports are still emerging, but unlike as with other leaks, we cannot see the material for ourselves.

It also appears that the Mossack Fonseca Papers have signalled a battle between the traditional method of mega-leaks as exemplified by WikiLeaks, and that preferred by the ICIJ. 'We're not WikiLeaks,' said Gerard Ryle, the director of the ICIJ in *Wired* (4th April 2016), when he was asked why the entire leak had not been made public. 'We're trying to show that journalism can be done responsibly.' This provocation of WikiLeaks indicates a political emphasis at work in the ICIJ, who should at the very least be supportive of an organisation like WikiLeaks, although maybe not after WikiLeaks responded to this defamation by tweeting that the ICIJ was a 'Washington DC based Ford, Soros funded soft-power tax-dodge' with 'a WikiLeaks problem' (Twitter, 5th April 2016).

Lawyer and journalist Chase Madar, author of *The Passion of Chelsea Manning* (2013), responded to this initial smear of WikiLeaks and called it 'obnoxious', adding that 'WikiLeaks has overall done a terrific job and done the world a great service.' (Twitter, 5th April 2016).

The result in the case of the Mossack Fonseca Papers is still mixed however, with one blogger on the website Off-Guardian (4th April 2016) summing it up as 'a list of geo-political nobodies, has-beens, easy targets and dead ancestors.' To top this off it appears that the majority of the information in the Mossack Fonseca Papers will never be made public, leading an increasing number of independent reporters to suggest that there is a possibility that investigative journalism has in this instance been reduced to the publishing of billionaires' enemy lists under the guise of a leak.

Whatever the motives for the leak, the journalists working on the Mossack Fonseca material have been quick to highlight the activities of a curious collection of public figures like Jackie Chan, and the father of UK Prime Minister David Cameron. While this complies with the narrative that the rich do not pay their taxes (despite the Tax Foundation reporting that the top 1% of earners pay nearly 50% of federal taxes; CNBC, 14th April 2015) it also helped generate some idiotic headlines featuring Vladimir Putin (*The Guardian,* 3rd April 2016) and Bashar al-Assad (*The Independent*, 4th April 2016).

As ever, the press are expected to play a most crucial role in making sense of our information, verifying its authenticity, and delivering it as impartially as possible, and free from the casual smears and spins which are the norm.

It's what most would agree journalists are supposed to do, even if, as in the case of Barrett Brown, they are unable to do it because they are locked up for their efforts. It remains to be seen what the fallout from the Mossack Fonseca Papers will be, but so far it has amounted to numerous bruised reputations, and a boost for the tax-trickery and legal side-stepping that's now on the rise in a handful of American states.

CHAPTER 6 WE ARE THE UNCONCERNED

How and Why to Gain Privacy

> While it's illegal to use Brad Pitt's image to sell a watch without his permission, Facebook is free to use your name to sell one to your friends.
>
> Eli Pariser

Internet privacy is not purely the concern of the paranoid, although it is often presented this way. The data we generate in our electronic communications is an historical agglomeration that's invisible to ourselves but when correctly collated forms a useful picture of who we are. Although privacy activism tends to focus on the government use and collection of this data, there are more obvious and permitted methods of data acquisition – those that run for commercial purpose.

By some measures, surveillance increases human individuality and does not erode it. Moreover, none of these questions are new to our era even if we behave as if they are. Karl Marx discussed the control of workers through observation in order to maximise labour processes, and even before the Internet was fully conceived, thinkers such as Frederick Taylor (1947) had written on the monitoring and reporting of working life, while Anthony Giddens argued that we must in general resist the temptation to assume surveillance is altogether a negative thing. In fact, Giddens has argued that surveillance may be an essential component of modernity and that it is basic for both social control, and for the gaining and exercise of liberties. Surveillance as we understand it today, however, extends to the observation of terrorists, alleged terrorists, the families and friends of alleged terrorists, and anyone who says mean things on the Internet.

Surveillance then can be both a good or bad thing, but the point at which it impinges on the material conditions of life is important, as are the reasons behind it. When we talk about *our own information* we should occasionally ask ourselves what we consider our information to be. If we buy an item and the purchase is recorded, what aspect of the process is ours and what belongs the retailer?

Privacy can therefore be attached to many things in order to articulate an interest – a little like the word security – and whistle-blowers and journalists can be criminalised in this debate, although there have also been cases in which citizens and private companies have been prosecuted for supplying encryption services. Fallout from the Edward Snowden case for example brought wider attention to an email service called Lavabit in July 2013 when it was revealed that Snowden had used a Lavabit email address to invite human rights lawyers and activists to a press conference during his confinement at Sheremetyevo International Airport in Moscow.

Lavabit was an encrypted email service that began in 2004 in reaction to privacy concerns about Google's practice of scanning the content of users' Gmail messages to generate advertisements and marketing data. The first that Lavabit heard about their own particular legal difficulties was the day after Snowden revealed his identity, when the US federal government served them a court order asking for metadata on a customer who was unnamed. Although the timing and circumstances suggested that Snowden was this customer, the federal government quickly obtained a search warrant demanding that Lavabit give away the private encryption keys to its entire service, an action which would have affected all Lavabit users. As he was unwilling to hand over these encryption keys, the company's owner Ladar Levison shut down the service months later and prepared to face many years of state persecution. In 2016, a redaction error on behalf of the government confirmed that Edward Snowden was the target (*Wired*, 17th March 2016) and in January 2017, Levison felt once more able to recommence his business, and lavabit.com returned.

Lavabit, like other encrypted email services, employs encryption technology on its server. It provides an encrypted bridge between the user's home computer and the server, and this allows Lavabit to secure people's communications without changing any of the email protocols that have been in place since the 1970s. In a sense, this model no longer works, and it looks like future technologies will look at pushing encryption down to a person's computer and so remove it from email and other service providers. This means that in the future, to avoid anybody taking advantage of our data, information will be encrypted on our devices and sent specifically to another party that only they can decrypt.

Ladar Levison said himself in *The Guardian*, in May 2014: 'My legal saga started last summer with a knock at the door, behind which stood two federal agents ready to serve me with a court order requiring the installation of surveillance equipment on my company's network.' He went on to say that he had no option but to install the equipment, which would allow the US government access to all his messages, but when he was asked for the encryption keys that would allow the government all his users' passwords, he drew the line. 'What ensued,' he said, 'was a flurry of legal proceedings that would last 38 days, ending not only my start-up but also destroying, bit by bit, the very principle upon which I founded it – that we all have a right to personal privacy.' The Lavabit story underlines several points. While the prosecution argued that Lavabit's users had no expectation of privacy, Lavabit argued that its service was specifically designed to this end. Levison's issue was not that he was unwilling to share data with the authorities, and we know this because he had delivered on all previous search warrants and requests that had been made of him. The issue was that the authorities had demanded the details of all of Lavabit's customers under one warrant. The larger legal question raised by this case was whether law enforcement can demand the encryption keys of a business and use those keys to inspect the private communications of every customer of that business, even when the court has only authorised them to access information belonging to specific targets.

In the same *Guardian* article, Levison concluded: 'If we allow our government to continue operating in secret, it is only a matter of time before you or a loved one find yourself in a position like I did – standing in a secret courtroom, alone, and without any of the meaningful protections that were always supposed to be the people's defence against an abuse of the state's power.'

Whereas some technologists have knowingly skirted the grey areas between legal and illegal, Ladar Levison was offering an email service that he hoped would deliver a certain privacy against advertisers who were collecting marketing data. However, what transpired is that Levison and his service were criminalised and the notion of such personal privacy as he offered was most definitely quashed. The goal of Levison's service was to remove the service provider from the surveillance system, insofar as while messages were stored on the Lavabit server, they would be protected, and what the government wished to do was access those messages before they were encrypted. Levison's own concern with this was that it was going to be carried out indiscriminately and with no transparency. He was also worried that with the encryption keys in their pocket, the intelligence services would be able to masquerade as Lavabit online.

One of the most fascinating questions about the Lavabit case is whether or not the average person even cares about privacy – indeed, our preoccupation with Facebook would suggest that we do not. Privacy can be defined in several ways but broadly speaking most people would define it as relating to their retaining control over what other people learn about them. It is the hope of Ladar Levison and those like him that a new set of standards and technologies will return that control to users. So far however, governments have failed to set the bar for what is right in terms of surveillance, and so it is down to the public to make it known what they wish their taxes being spent on.

The story of Aaron Swartz (1986-2013) is fully told in the documentary *The Internet's Own Boy* (Brian Knappenberger, 2014) which shows how a talented American computer programmer, entrepreneur, writer, political organiser and activist came to commit suicide after what many consider to be undue prosecution – and persecution – by the FBI.

Swartz's achievements in his short life were significant. He was involved in the development of the web feed format RSS and the Markdown publishing format, as well as the organisation and implementation of Creative Commons, which is now used widely as a user-friendly adjunct to copyright. Swartz was also a part of the team that set up Reddit – and these are only some of his better-known achievements. But Aaron Swartz was a popular and principled activist, as well as teacher and friend to many.

In all, Swartz was an exceptionally positive force on the Internet, and was interested in how the World Wide Web could help people as a whole. A fine example took place in 2008, when Swartz downloaded about 2.7 million federal court documents stored in the PACER (Public Access to Court Electronic Records) database and made them publicly available outside of the expensive service offered by the Administrative Office of the United States Courts. Although this action brought Swartz to the attention of the FBI, charges were never pressed because the documents were of course public. The upshot of this is significant enough when you consider that PACER still charges the public to obtain the documents – per page – while many of these same public documents are now openly available to anyone with a free browser plug in called RECAP, which allows citizens to search for and download not only what they need – but what is also already theirs.

Aside from programming, Aaron Swartz's work focused on civic awareness and activism, and at the age of 24, in 2010, he became a research fellow at Harvard University's Safra Research Lab on Institutional Corruption. Swartz also founded the online group Demand Progress, known for its successful campaign against the Stop Online Piracy Act (SOPA).

Intimidation and prosecutorial attacks finally got the better of Aaron Swartz after he was arrested for downloading academic journal articles from JSTOR ('Journal Storage') at MIT after breaking into a computer closet on the premises. Federal prosecutors later charged Swartz with two counts of wire fraud and eleven violations of the Computer Fraud and Abuse Act, all of which carried a combined maximum penalty of $1 million in fines, and 35 years in prison.

Facing potential incarceration for alleged criminal offenses for which the victims (MIT and JSTOR) even declined to pursue civil litigation, Swartz died by suicide on January 11th, 2013.

In his short life, Aaron Swartz sought progressive change, especially in his native North America, and he went head to head with some of the most significant powers on the planet. The issues of copyright law, freedom of expression, and open access were dear to him and even though he is hugely missed by the community of activists and technologists to which he belonged, his work continues most notably in the form of the Electronic Frontier Foundation (EFF) a non-profit digital rights group, which was established in 1990.

In recent years the Electronic Frontier Foundation has analysed the practices of major Internet companies and service providers, judging their publicly available policies and highlighting best practices. Since commencing this reporting in 2010, the EFF have seen a transformation take place, and the best practices they identified in their early reports have become industry standards. The EFF are now monitoring a series of industry-accepted customs that cover the use of your data, the level of access the government has to this data, and the general transparency when it comes to what they are doing with it.

It so appears that given the reinvigorated debate over encryption, companies must now take a public position against the compelled inclusion of deliberate security weaknesses or other back doors in their software and servers, and given how fast things are changing, the EFF expect these categories to continue to evolve, so that public confidence may be regained across a range of privacy issues.

The value of our information to, in particular, the corporations of the world, cannot be underestimated, and data companies have proliferated in recent years, selling information in a variety of ways. The data, often packaged as something like 'audience propensities' and offering 'multidimensional insights' is becoming more complex by the day and is now subject to widespread analysis by artificial intelligence. When Microsoft set about purchasing LinkedIn in 2016, the $26 billion suggested value of LinkedIn was based largely on the worth of the 433 million members and 2 million paid subscribers. Microsoft itself has more than 1.2 billion Office users, but it has no social service and so it has previously had to rely on Facebook and others to provide human beings' personal data. In the same way that just about all our children play Minecraft (also acquired by Microsoft), it's safe to assume that a large percentage of adults use

LinkedIn for work-related networking or communicating with colleagues and so forth. As artificial intelligence is the way that our information is now processed, and because it has such huge capacities, better results will be achieved with greater amounts of information.

A typical marketing technology company will offer customer information divided into up to 10,000 fields, each with a specific aspect about you. One field may assess your political tendencies, while another will state whether you prefer a diet soft drink or its 'full-fat' variant – while another will state whether you are homosexual or not. Further, this data is constantly assessed for its accuracy, and each data field will come with a source, whether it be Facebook or an online questionnaire. The information is now so valuable in fact, that separate so-called data cleaning companies have sprung up, verifying and checking this information – all of it legally collected. This data will always be gathered in spite of ourselves and even if we're not worried about the government spying on us, we should probably at least wish to minimise the all-engulfing effect of our online footprints. It is increasingly difficult to opt out of data systems, and it is inevitable that mass amounts of photographs and information about us will remain long after we have gone, although while we are here they are immensely useful for predicting our behaviour.

One of the principal items of software used to collate information is the browser cookie. A cookie is a small text file that is stored on your device when you visit a website, and only the owner of that website will be able to retrieve or read the contents of that cookie. Each cookie is unique to your web browser and will contain an identifier which will allow the website which served it to remember things about what you are doing. In 2010, a major website may have placed on average five cookies on your computer during a visit, but now that number can be many times that – and this will include files from ad servers, data brokers, and other third-party companies that will pay to have them there.

Scandalously, cookies in Facebook 'like' buttons on other websites across the Internet are able to track Facebook users across most other websites even when they are not logged in, and the company can also use data to make inferences about non-Facebook users using a process it calls 'lookalike' targeting (*Wall Street Journal,* 27th May 2016). The future potential in this field is without limit and consequently irresistible to programmers and marketers.

Another current matter is the rise of cloud storage. You have probably worked out by now that there is no 'data cloud' – there is just the Internet – but now more than ever we store everything remotely on Google, Microsoft, Amazon and IBM servers – those are the four largest operators at least. Current estimates vary, but it appears that about 30% of consumer content is now stored by cloud-computing providers, and depressingly, because legislation is still a distant dream, this information belongs to the online services in question, and not the user. The 'cloud-computing wars' (as *The Economist* called them in an article 'Cloud Chronicles', August 2016) have begun in earnest, and they proceed quite candidly placing profit over privacy. 'The latest battleground is data,' *The Economist* article states. 'Cloud providers are hoovering up digital information left and right so they can mine it and use it for insights to offer new services or improve existing ones.' The greatest winner in this battle so far is Amazon Web Services (AWS), which according to the same article has ten times as much computing capacity as the next 14 cloud providers combined, and with profits in this business being far greater than anyone imagined, the momentum for this kind of computing and for AWS to grow is immense.

We may be knee-deep in grey areas but the false trade-off is always the same: people are happy to use these services that they don't pay for because they know that the material they are uploading can be assessed and used by the company that owns the server. This doesn't mean that any of these services are going to take a picture of your cat and run it in an advertisement, claiming it is theirs. What they do use the photos for, among other things, is gaining other information such as where you go, who you hang with, which devices you use, how often you take photographs, what sort of cat food your furry friend likes – and more.

In the case of the many bloggers who use Wordpress it is with the blackest of humour, for example, that we sometimes see these blog-writers copyrighting their material as if Automattic – the company that owns Wordpress – are so philanthropic as to offer free software and hosting. There is in fact no debate about who owns the material on a Wordpress blog because it is stated in the Automattic Terms of Service that they have royalty-free access to your data:

> By submitting Content to Automattic for inclusion on your website, you grant Automattic a world-wide, royalty-free, and non-exclusive license to reproduce, modify, adapt and publish the Content solely for the purpose of displaying, distributing, and promoting your blog. This license allows Automattic to make publicly-posted content available to third parties selected by Automattic so that these third parties can analyse and distribute your content through their services. If you delete Content, Automattic will use reasonable efforts to remove it from wordpress.com, but you acknowledge that caching or references to the Content may not be made immediately unavailable.

Our current generation may one day be historically held as the most careless with its data. In fact, I hold it in this regard already. Google has a decade of browsing history for somewhere between 90 and 95 percent of computer users in the UK and this includes data on what we've searched, what we've bought, which sites we've visited, who our friends are, and more. This is not to suggest that Google or anybody else is set to do anything malign with this information because even Google don't know what they are going to do with it, and what shape it will take or use it could be put to.

As laws vary from territory to territory, and as no member of the public can be entirely sure what access law enforcement and marketing companies have to the information, it would appear that it is safe to assume that we cannot in any way protect ourselves against anything we upload being accessed by somebody else.

This is the bottom line hit we must stomach as users and losers in the war on privacy. It is usually noted by Google and other web services that data is anonymised. This means that the collected data has been stripped of any identifying factors, such as our names and locations. However, there is so much data available about ourselves that this point is moot, as each data set (or person) is now so complete that real anonymisation is virtually impossible, even though a UK Data Protection Bill will make un-anonymisation (if that concept makes sense to you) illegal.

The next thing to consider is that our information is routinely scanned for evidence or suggestions of crime. Our governments have made this a priority even though the exact definitions of what they are looking for are not fixed. Even so, information is scanned in aggregate, and with face recognition being one of the fastest developing technologies in this field, attention has turned again to Facebook which has gathered the most useful public cache of face-identifying data thanks to our propensity for tagging ourselves and others on its platform. Even non-users of Facebook have their face-prints in Facebook's database – a resource which seeks to be able to understand electronically what a person looks like from many different angles. The tagging software in Facebook is presented as an aid to help users find friends but when a company sells our data to third parties, data associated with images may be included. If the sanctity of your data on any given website is uncertain, then it's easy to imagine how less certain this may be as your data passes from one company to another, as it inevitably must.

Once again this information is not necessarily private. Much of it is public and has been shown to be more revealing than we might imagine through the experiments of Alessandro Acquisti and those like him (see Chapter Three), which have shown that huge amounts can be determined from a public CCTV system, including the home addresses, political affiliations and national security numbers of random passers-by. Governments have also started putting this private data to work and have reviewed or requested Facebook data for citizenship applications, criminal cases, and security checks. Even without warrants, as private detectives and security experts will testify, Facebook data contains far better information than the traditional police mug shot – and this is not just a concern because it opens doors for governments and firms, but because it is facilitates stalking and similar crimes.

My favourite recent example of how vulnerable we have become to abuse of data, simply by the fact of its existence, is a project carried out by Anthony Russell. In a proposal Russell titles 'Converting the Voter Database and Facebook into a Google for Criminals', Russell describes how he made a proof of concept app that took the Ohio voter database and positively linked this voter record to Facebook, which was accurate 45% of the time. This means, he says, that if the voter database he has contains 6.5 million records, he feels confident about extrapolating 2.86 million records by matching them with Facebook.

Now while you may already be comfortable that your own and several foreign governments have already done this with your Facebook luggage, Anthony Russell is asking us to consider what private individuals and companies may be able to do. The process is quite understandable, even to people with limited technological knowledge, but it begins with the public electoral roll, which contains the first name, last name, date of birth and home address of everybody above age.

'To start,' he writes, 'I had to see what public data was available. In short, there's a ton. No wonder we get marketed nonstop by mail. The government takes our personal information and puts it on the web for free. Write a couple of scripts and you can tap it anytime.'

To begin with, and even without writing such

scripts, which may very well be illegal anyway, Russell simply accessed his state's voter records, which contained the above details of 6.5 million people in a straightforward CSV (comma separated value) file which could be opened by any spreadsheet program, such as Microsoft Excel.

What Russell did then, he does not exactly say, and for good reason. Because when he began experimenting with these records and made the same basic Facebook queries again and again, to find people in a certain area, he began to get matches. His search however was fairly simple, and looked something like this: https://www.facebook.com/search/people/?q=FIRST+LAST+STATE.

Once he had generated a list of potential matching profiles, Russell then says he began scrubbing them and generating confidence scores, to predict the accuracy of any given result. Using the names, dates of birth and addresses that he had accessed publicly, he could then generate a match and have his software routine present a confidence score that this profile match was accurate.

Russell presented his redacted script in *2600*, and wrote: 'I was able to run this script over thousands of people without getting rate limited by Facebook. Conceivably, I could run this nonstop and eventually build a giant database.'

Such a process could leverage all sorts of data which we might imagine is private, but which is commonly attainable. It could offer all kinds of information, such as all the people that work for a specific company, or all the elderly people in a certain area, information on groups, families and public services, including their personnel. It could also target people by interest, and be used for highly effective marketing, or indeed any of many criminal abuses.

Russell concludes: 'If I had the ear of the state IT rep, I would start there. I'd tell them that allowing anyone to download the entire voter database is probably a dumb idea. I understand why voter records are public and it's for a good reason. That said... the government just enabled me to build a Google for criminal enterprises. Facebook should also probably be limiting the above queries.'

The billions of images that Facebook has collected could be even more valuable to identity thieves and other indictable modern villains than any of this information however, and at present, much of what we understand and legislate about it is still in philosophical and legal limbo. Beginning in 2015, Facebook, Google, Shutterfly and Snapchat were (and are still being) sued under Illinois biometrics law. While Shutterfly settled confidentially, the others battled on with Google arguing that photographs were not covered by the local biometrics laws, while Facebook argued that the case should be thrown out because the users who are suing them have not suffered any concrete injury such as physical harm, loss of money or property.

Activists including those at the EFF have argued that prior permission should be required from people before they are identified by faceprint technology and that as a base minimum, people should be able to move in public without the concern that agents unknown to them are tracking them or trying to work out who they are (*The Guardian,* 17th June 2015). Out of interest, these agents unknown in the case of Facebook are known to be the firm face.com, which they acquired in 2012. It seems however that basic safeguards are not going to be achievable in the war on privacy and that advances in technology, including the use of public drones and super-high-resolution cameras, will make identifying individuals in public places exceptionally easy. None of this is terribly far away, if it is not here already. Car registration plate recognition is widely in use, and time, place and person indices already exist which link vehicles with personal activity – a fact that raises questions about the use of faceprints.

Questions regarding this faceprint data might include:

- How long is this data kept?
- Who has access to it and under what circumstances?
- And how is it protected from abuse?

To these should be added questions concerning the nature of these so-called faceprints themselves. Since my faceprint is personally identifiable information, is it fair for me to ask if it is subject to data protection?

Already HD cameras are connected to public networks that allow individuals to be tracked while using public transport, shopping or participating in demonstrations. The most recent active versions of these systems can scan your face in real time and match it to information stored in a database. In common with your fingerprints your faceprint is a unique identifier, but unlike your fingertips, your face is easily viewable to the world and tends to be your most recognisable feature.

The complicated answer is that like your shopping habits, the faceprint is a sort of hybrid property that belongs to both you and the company or agency that collects it, and so it should be up to both of you in each case how it is used. In the meantime it is up to users to opt out of things like Facebook's Moments app which uses the social network's large database of human faces and information combined with artificial intelligence algorithms to recognise people by name in digital images. It doesn't appear to matter whether you are on Facebook or not, as it's now known that Facebook are working with other consumer data companies to compile profiles of as many humans as they can, including those who have never used any of their services (Belgian Privacy Commission, March 2015).

Finally, location data may be considered. Of course, it's your mobile phone which most commonly records your movements, but new location revealing devices are released every year and you'd be advised to be cautious about anything that has the word 'smart' in its name. The two-edged sword when it comes to location data is that legislation is weak when it comes to both the gathering of it and its general accessibility. One reason for the lack of regulation concerning location data is because information gathered this way is so massively useful to law enforcement – much more so than your shopping habits – and so there is a large amount of resistance when it comes to privacy laws in this area.

Snowden himself discussed this in a TED Talk, arguing that if we continue to allow technology to be used on the basis that most of us have nothing to hide, we are in effect giving up our rights. 'Your rights matter,' he said, 'because you never know when you're going to need them.'

Most vexing is the fact that in coming late to this debate we have allowed complete transparency to become our considered default when it comes to privacy, with the general repercussion being that attempts to conceal your data are seen as either paranoid or criminal.

I would therefore like to introduce a few privacy tools that may be used at home; some are basic and others are more complicated. It is legitimate to seek to protect your information and remain anonymous and nothing we read or hear should attempt to persuade us otherwise. This is because the marketing intelligence we provide for free or as part of our ISP's Terms and Conditions, without Edward Snowden having to risk his life, is more damaging than the possibility of our governments stockpiling our phone data and browsing history.

Yes, the activity of GCHQ and the NSA challenges principles concerning what is to be considered right and good. But when it comes to the information we are giving away for free – the times when we waive our privacy and offer up our preferences without a thought – these are the truly damaging leaks in our current macrocosm.

Although it's in their interests to say so, the companies which deal in our data maintain that we are much more willing to share it with them than we used to be. Acxiom Corporation (ACXM), a recognised leader in enterprise data and analytics have on their website a report from a group called The Future Foundation, which argues:

> The data driven economy is undoubtedly the engine of growth and the driver of value in this information age. It is therefore crucial that brand strategists, futurologists and government regulators keep up to date with fast changing attitudes to privacy... [our] study shows a considerable change in attitudes since 2012, with significant increases overall in those willing to share data and a significant decrease in fundamentalists opposed to sharing data.

Observe how this marketing firm styles those who do not share their data as 'fundamentalists' – a smear they couple with the implication that as far as they are concerned, people are giving consent for their data to be gathered simply by using the Internet. Here, the language of data protection expresses the values the industry wishes to express. Data fundamentalists are 'those who are unwilling to exchange personal information, regardless of any enhanced service they may receive in return' and individuals are presented by such companies in their literature as somehow being enemies of progress.

As with others in this field, Acxiom argue that the public are increasingly open to using their personal information in order to work out better deals, and that the fastest growing group in their own UK surveys constitute a demographic they refer to as The Unconcerned – who in 2015 made up 22% of those they polled. It is possible that while I rail against the cunning minds at the GCHQ and the NSA, that there are companies gaily trading in my information and collaborating to build complete commercial and social profiles of me. In fact, it's a given that this is happening, because we are somehow telling them that we are indeed as they wish to name us – The Unconcerned.

The average data company may have as many procedures and programs as the NSA. A single relatively modest data solutions company will offer a range of services including Passenger Insight (targeting travellers); improvement in Customer Acquisition by means of segmentation and recognition; Data Onboarding, which matches offline customer records with online activity, and thus circumvents data anonymisation; Audience Propensities; Purchase Propensities and Affordability Data, which will show who can afford what you are offering. Many of the same insight techniques predict who might be a customer and integrate multi-dimensional factors such as 'why' customers act the way they do and 'how' they may behave in the future – presumably on a similar basis to the way the GCHQ attempt to predict who may be a criminal.

The marketing uses of data are not to be conflated with security issues, but there are similarities that would be of interest to a public who have not traditionally been used to debating privacy. I would disagree with Acxiom's assertion that we are happier than ever to share information, especially when public sensitivity to issues around data security are at an unprecedented level – and I am not sure here if I'd like to say this is an unprecedentedly low level, given what we know. The public presumably remain unconcerned until a significant outrage sways opinion, while at present, the most significant outrages are terrorist, which of course sway opinion towards total transparency.

As consumers we've not traditionally bothered with privacy, a fact obvious insofar as there is not yet any simple way to discuss it. But technologies that were initially created for freedom, as modelled in Aldous Huxley's 1932 novel *Brave New World*, can end up becoming coercive and controlling. In the case of the data we generate, we seem unsure as a society of its purpose, and yet still feel a necessity to store it. One might ask if the data we are stockpiling about ourselves online can be used for any good at all?

For personal security there are a few measures you can take – some simple, some less so. It remains to be seen how long it will be before we have established Internet-wide encryption, but we can be certain that data collection will never cease. There are however plenty browser plug-ins which are available and other services which allow us to keep a check on these matters. Such as:

StartPage

By switching my Internet search engine to StartPage I have ensured that Google will still be able to collect data about searches that I make, but that these searches will not point back to me as an individual. It's a small thing, but the difference is significant. Google can still track me when I am browsing because their analytics are embedded on most websites – but at least they cannot see the searches I make and compound that with other data they hold about me.

Lightbeam

Lightbeam is available free for Firefox and takes a second to plug into your browser. When operational, Lightbeam shows you the sites that you have navigated to, alongside the sites that are tracking you that you have not navigated to. The idea here is that somewhere, presumably in the terms and conditions you will not read, you have consented to all of these services tracking your activity. However, when you see how many websites are following you, you will be surprised!

Running Lightbeam for a week I saw that I had navigated through choice to 52 sites, but I had actually accessed 372 websites that had placed cookies on my computer and were collecting information. These are easily distinguished by the plug-in which identifies the third-party sites that are tracking me.

Some of these third-party sites are innocent, but on the whole the other ones – which can be hard to identify even if you can read their names – are collecting information, although it's not always clear for whom.

Gary Kovacs, the CEO of Mozilla, presented Lightbeam in 2012 and continues to develop the program. 'Privacy is not an option and shouldn't be the price we accept for just getting on the Internet,' he says.

And he is right. The technical controls required to meet the balance between security and privacy are now available, and while nobody will deny marketing companies the right to collect the information they need to make our experience better, clarity and openness will be needed if we are to save ourselves from becoming slaves to our growing datasets.

TOR

It used to be the case that online privacy could be, for all practical purposes, achieved with a browser called TOR (The Onion Router).

TOR is a web browser that connects to a network of proxy Internet addresses. A proxy is another computer that acts as a hub through which Internet requests are processed. By connecting through these proxies, TOR users have an intermediary between their computer and the rest of the Internet. Proxies can be used to filter web content, get around restrictions such as parental blocks, to assess downloads and uploads for safety, and to provide anonymity. This is because all subsequent records of TOR browsing will not be traced to the user but to the address of the proxy.

TOR can be difficult to operate and on balance is probably not worth the effort. For the curious, however, TOR delivers access to special Internet networks that normal browsers cannot, a collection of networks normally known as the Dark Web. On the TOR network are blogs that may otherwise suffer from censorship, a plethora of weird sites that exist for curiosity, and a whole lot of pages run by bad guys, which are usually obnoxious and/or illegal. Legal authorities and others also run honeypot websites on this network in order to capture wrongdoers.

In 2011 the hacker group Anonymous launched a project called Operation Darknet which targeted child pornography sites on the TOR network. Thanks to these anons, hundreds of these sites were damaged and membership lists, which included home addresses, were passed to the authorities. The FBI have also been involved in shutting down child pornography on the TOR network by creating an exploit which returned to them details of TOR users, and they successfully identified the individual behind one of the largest hosting sites on the network in September 2013. Incidentally, a training presentation disclosed by Edward Snowden showed the codename for the exploit – EGOTISTICALGIRAFFE.

Although its reputation may now be unsavoury, TOR was originally created by the US Navy's tech laboratories in order to secure the transfer of information between two locations. In practise TOR uses a range of proxy servers, and this is not a bad thing, because nowadays connecting to any site can potentially let dozens of other sites know exactly where and who you are. Security provided by TOR is not complete, however, and those planning to use the TOR browser for accessing illegal content should reflect upon this. Law enforcement is still concerned with criminality and will focus on catching anyone accessing illegal services, and TOR users are not safe from them. However, for those inquisitive about the Dark Web, TOR is useful.

A range of advice on these and other matters is available from the Electronic Frontier Foundation on the website privacytools.io where you'll find a sizeable selection of browser add-ons for content control, self-destructing cookies, and for privacy. One add-on called Disconnect, built in 2011 by former Google engineers and a privacy-rights attorney, disables tracking by third party sites and consequently opens your webpages faster, while also keeping your searches private. An add-on like this is great because while your browser is communicating with third-party sites, your webpages are taking longer to load. Users of Disconnect have seen this for themselves and report that their browser speed is increased by up to 30%.

Also listed on privacytools.io are privacy-conscious email providers (mostly in Europe, where laws are more relaxed); encrypted messaging, email and cloud services; and decentralised social networks, which allow users to control their content insofar as while it is shared with friends, it is never shared with the host company.

The EFF recommend that consumers do not use services based in the United States because of the surveillance programs we have discussed, as well as the US government's use of National Security Letters (NSLs). A National Security Letter is an administrative subpoena issued by the United States federal government to gather information for national security purposes, but crucially, because they are a security tool, NSLs do not require prior approval from a judge.

On top of this, NSLs are usually applied with a gag order, which forbids the recipient from talking about any requests. This combination allows the government to secretly force companies to grant access to customer data and transform the service into a tool of mass surveillance.

The final thought from the Electronic Frontier Foundation is that computer users consider not using the world's second most popular operating system, Windows, because it allows Microsoft (which owns it) to log everything, from a user's Wi-Fi password, to their contacts, interests, habits, calendar data, credit card information, emails, audio and video recordings, browser history and keystrokes.

Good as Windows is, all of its usage information is exchanged between our computers and Microsoft's data centres – where it will doubtless still reside long after we have passed on.

The website privacytools.io states:

> In downloading Windows 10, you are authorizing Microsoft to share any of above mentioned data with any third-party, with or without your consent – it's one of these statements that are too overwhelming to comprehend and which offers implications beyond what you can imagine outwith science fiction. It is without doubt a concern and something to bear in mind, because the data will long outlive you.

Other operating systems are available.

CHAPTER 7 FUTURE FAMILIAR?

Encryption and the Blockchain

> I'm very sympathetic to attempts to increase security against organised crime, but you have to distinguish yourself from the criminal.
>
> Tim Berners-Lee

This statement was made by Tim Berners-Lee in response to the news as revealed by Edward Snowden that US and UK spy agencies had been working to crack encrypted data. Given the value and proliferation of information it is likely that one of the next areas of growth will be in encryption. 'Crypto' (that which is hidden) refers to the use of codes, paired with technology to create systems that are immune to spying. As we have seen, a proportion of Internet traffic is completely visible. While computers and user accounts are password protected, data on the move is often not encrypted meaning that those with the means can access it.

The hope for encryption is that the decentralised nature of the Internet will secure our privacy and ensure that more data than ever will be encrypted, both at rest and on the move. This is certain to happen because when it was first conceived, the Internet offered no such confidentiality. With our increased overall security, we will also need to re-examine our laws and customs.

There is a legal nicety called the Third-Party Doctrine, which in North America translates to the idea that you will lose your Fourth Amendment rights when you relinquish information to a third party. This has in the past been interpreted to mean that in giving up your data to an organisation such as a telecoms company or an email provider, you lose any right to expect privacy as far as that data is concerned. The ruling that covers this has been updated several times in recent decades.

Of course, when the Fourth Amendment was drafted, the large amount of people's private activity went on inside their homes, so it made sense at that time to make the household the focus for these. The use of smartphones, the Internet and credit cards means that these rights don't make as much sense as they once did. As it stands then, Americans have no protection against warrantless government access to bank records, telephony and many other facets of daily life. One recent Supreme Court decision on this matter (United States v. Jones, 2012) involved GPS tracking performed directly by the government, without a third-party intermediary. The government lost this case as it hinged on their intruding on a person's private property, although the judge in the case took the opportunity to express some doubt regarding the current implementation of the Third-Party Doctrine as it stands today, saying:

This approach is ill suited to the digital age, in which people reveal a great deal of information about themselves to third parties in the course of carrying out mundane tasks.

(*The Atlantic*, 30th December 2013)

The Third-Party Doctrine may be an American legal consideration, but UK and world users must not think that it does not apply to them. The fact is that most of the Internet traffic in the world passes through American servers, so it is something we should all think about.

Although it was far from being a priority in the first decade of the twenty-first century, large companies are now adopting encryption technologies faster than ever, a move accelerated by the fact that encryption is increasingly becoming a selling point. Both Apple and Google are building encryption into messaging and everything else on their phones, and there is also now a device called a Blackphone, which is a privacy-built smartphone which runs a modified version of Android called SilentOS and comes with a package of security-minded tools.

I feel that there is a sufficient amount of data the public should have routinely encrypted and some of these are even required by law to be private. These include bank statements, contracts, confidentiality agreements, job offers, financial records, medical histories, and lab test results. For those keen to activate email privacy, the Pretty Good Privacy program (PGP) is a good place to start. While PGP won't guarantee preventing a major government from cracking your mail, it can certainly protect you from corporate tracking, just as it will prevent employers reading personal emails and keep identity thieves and hackers off your back. Of these, the main one to be aware of is what comes under the bracket of corporate snooping, because you may have unwittingly opted into something like this when you signed up for free email, and are now being targeted with ads for new furniture, just because you asked a friend in an email where she got her new settee. Once more, it's not the government that are planning to ruin your day but the more mundane elements on the Internet, such as the marketing machine churning in the background.

On the other hand, if you are a corporation and don't encrypt and secure your data, you are in potentially far greater trouble – and this is why the conversation regarding security of our information comes first nowadays, even before profit and functionality in some cases.

In a move that would have seemed unthinkable before the Snowden revelations, Apple's CEO Tim Cook published a letter on apple.com on 16 February 2016, which began:

> The United States government has demanded that Apple take an unprecedented step which threatens the security of our customers. We oppose this order, which has implications far beyond the legal case at hand.

The letter went on to state that the FBI asked the firm to build a backdoor into their popular product, the iPhone. This request, which came about as a part of investigations into the murderous San Bernardino attacks of 2015, brought information about encryption helpfully further into public view. Cook continued:

> Specifically, the FBI wants us to make a new version of the iPhone operating system, circumventing several important security features... In the wrong hands, this software – which does not exist today – would have the potential to unlock any iPhone in someone's physical possession. The FBI may use different words to describe this tool, but make no mistake: Building a version of iOS that bypasses security in this way would undeniably create a backdoor. And while the government may argue that its use would be limited to this case, there is no way to guarantee such control.

The letter from Apple not only shamed the US federal government and its attempts to circumvent security, but made a good play insofar as it showed that Apple is working for the security of its customers. What Apple are implying in this communication is that if their products became less secure, their market share would collapse as American phones would be viewed globally as sub-standard.

'The government is asking Apple to hack our own users and undermine decades of security advancements that protect our customers,' said Tim Cook's communiqué, '– including tens of millions of American citizens – from sophisticated hackers and cybercriminals. The same engineers who built strong encryption into the iPhone to protect our users would, ironically, be ordered to weaken those protections and make our users less safe.'

The issue here is not just the encryption of private data, but the encryption of the data of a mass murderer, and it came about because the phone in question was built with far superior encryption in an effort to meet increasing demand for privacy from the public. In the wake of this request, people who know what they are talking about, such as Edward Snowden, Google CEO Sundar Pichai, and Twitter CEO Jack Dorsay, spoke in defence of Apple, while politicians both liberal and conservative argued for Apple to relent.

The FBI-Apple encryption dispute came to a sudden and unusual ending in March 2016 after Apple declined to create the software and a hearing was scheduled. However, a day before the hearing was supposed to happen, the government obtained a delay, saying they had found a third party to assist in unlocking the iPhone and, on March 28th, it announced that the FBI had with the help of an Israeli firm, unlocked the San Bernardino iPhone, and they withdrew their request.

Many of our technological concerns, including identity theft, fraud, financial theft, corruption, surveillance and hacking can be met by the use of encryption, and it is telling that our governments are not open about this. It is wrong to suggest that if an insecure operating system was specially constructed for private government use it would never be abused by hackers, leakers, blackmailers or any number of other individuals who might help place the keys to such a system on the black market. Although there have been similar cases to the Apple-FBI encryption dispute, Apple's public response shone a spotlight on developers who provide free-market solutions to the public's legitimate requests for safety.

Despite this, governments continue to, and will continue to, call for limits to the public's access to non-backdoored encryption. In a move reminiscent of the Clipper Chip of 1996, UK Prime Minister David Cameron previously called for outlawing non-backdoored cryptography, saying that there should be 'no means of communication which we cannot read.' (BBC News, 13th January 2015).

The name for those who support crypto technology is cypherpunks – and while we have relied on hackers and whistle-blowers to let us know what is being collected in our names, it is the cypherpunks who are the architects of the future. Notable cypherpunks who we have already met in this book are Julian Assange and Jacob Appelbaum – but you will hear more from this brand of activist in coming years, as many of them respond to the public's need for security from criminals, corporate data trackers, and from those who were in the first place supposed to be protecting us. What is encouraging is that the corporations appear to be at least partially on their side. As Edward Snowden showed us, intelligence agencies have been able to bypass encryption of data stored on Android and iOS smartphones by legally ordering Google and Apple to bypass the encryption on specific phones. But around 2014, as a reaction to this, Google and Apple redesigned their encryption so that spying agencies did not have the technical ability to bypass it, and that data could only be unlocked by the user's passcode.

Encryption is a key feature of one of the most significant Internet developments yet – the blockchain. While it is true that there could be no blockchain without the Internet, the blockchain may be far more powerful than the network that supports it. Most of us will know the blockchain through its primary application, which is the cryptocurrency (digital currency) known as bitcoin.

To grasp the concept of bitcoin, it's best to compare it to the kind of cash you carry around in your pocket. Cash transactions are peer-to-peer because they involve no middle-person, and a bitcoin transaction is the same. The difference is that with cash, users have physical items in the form of banknotes and coins to prove that the exchange has completed, whereas with bitcoin what we have to show that a transaction took place is a mathematically unforgettable record on a worldwide shared ledger.

The blockchain that makes bitcoin operate is a public ledger of all transactions, and it is this ledger that acts as the proof that a bitcoin transfer has been made. The genius of the blockchain is that it is a continuingly growing register of every bitcoin transaction and that it cannot be tampered with, even by its operators. This works because the blockchain includes in its public entries a time-stamp that precludes any bitcoin from being spent again.

The maths involved are mind-boggling. When you ask a bank how much money you have on deposit, the bank refers to a balance which only yourself and the bank can see and which is protected by the bank's own security infrastructures.

When you ask the blockchain for how much money you hold, your bitcoin software examines the entire ledger of encrypted transactions, beginning with the very first ever bitcoin transaction, and it calculates your balance by consulting the entire ledger, searching for your entries.

This is not only an inexpensive way of protecting your balance, but it is even more private than a bank because only you can see how much money you hold.

The blockchain and bitcoin are therefore only possible thanks to the power of the Internet, which distributes copies of the ledger across the world. At present, there are over 6,500 copies of the bitcoin ledger on computers around the world and no bitcoin transaction of any sort can take place unless all of these ledgers match. If any ledger were out by even one digit then the entire system would collapse, but so far it has been extremely successful – because it is private, cheap, and has no central authority.

Whereas a conventional financial ledger records the transfers of money from place to place, the bitcoin blockchain uses a time-stamp – a sequence of encoded information identifying when a certain event occurred, usually giving date and time of day, accurate to a small fraction of a second – as proof that value has been transferred from one place to another.

To explain what bitcoin is, it might also be better to explain how it could fail – because if somebody were to, for example, find a fault in the cryptography and devise a way of creating and issuing bitcoin by themselves, the entire value of bitcoin would disappear in a matter of hours. The same would apply if someone found a way of photocopying banknotes – their value would quickly reduce to nil.

So far however, blockchain technology has proved robust. The great thing about bitcoin, which makes it different from everything that has come before, is that there is no centralised point where something could miscarry. The number of bitcoins in the world – which is 21 million – does not matter – because that number can be divided endlessly, and this maintains much as gold did when currency was pegged to what was known as the gold standard.

Unfortunately, governments and banks have sometimes proved either incompetent or corrupt in the management of money, and discussion of the financial crisis still tends to come down to actual or perceived dishonesty and a belief that certain institutions are able to bend the system in their favour. At present, pension promises that are currently being made across the planet are already looking mathematically impossible to fulfil, and government spending and their creation of fiat currency – currency brought into being by legal decree as opposed to that pegged to a commodity such as gold – have us living in fear of another financial collapse. Consider the nations of the world's tax-to-debt ratios if you are not already sufficiently concerned about this.

Despite its promise, there are factors holding cryptocurrency back. One of these is that the technology is new, but there is also substantial political and corporate resistance. The financial industry in all its many and various manifestations is one of the largest industries in the world – The Organization for Economic Co-operation and Development (OECD) suggests that financial services typically make up 20-30% of total service market revenue and about 20% of the total gross domestic product in developed economies – all of which would be minimised by a cryptocurrency, which incurs virtually no transaction charges and requires no middle institution to validate and secure its operations.

In the meantime, there is hope that bitcoin could become a fully peer-to-peer decentralised and free to use global currency, although we should perhaps be sceptical of the fact that the very first iteration of cryptocurrency is going to be the one that we adopt and ends up being the most successful.

Bitcoin's biggest mystery is its creator. The first academic paper to propose bitcoin, called 'Bitcoin: A Peer-to-Peer Electronic Cash System' was published in November 2008 and is credited to an anonymous individual who identified as 'Satoshi Nakamoto'. There have been many attempts to out various people as Nakamoto, including press investigations, but nothing has proved conclusive, and thankfully the identity of the creator of bitcoin remains unknown. One of the more popular theories even connects the NSA to the creation of bitcoin, referring to the Agency's 1996 paper on the certain emergence of a cryptocurrency at some point in the future. One of the specialists referenced in this NSA paper is called Tatsuaki Okamoto, whom it is said, may have combined on the project with another scientist called Satoshi Obana – hence Satoshi Nakamoto.

I would like to argue that the fact that Satoshi Nakamoto certainly exists and is yet anonymous could be one of the validating factors in the success of bitcoin. It could also be true that the discovery of the identity of Nakamoto could damage the currency, when you consider how facts about high profile or influential people can affect market conditions. Using evidence in the blockchain itself, and examples in pseudonyms, stylometric analysis, ciphers and graphing the time stamps for each of Nakamoto's bitcoin forum posts, many curious individuals and groups have tried to locate Nakamoto, but so far nobody has proved anything regarding who this person is. Despite claims made by several individuals, there is currently no publicly available cryptographic proof that anyone in particular is bitcoin's creator.

As with other security and privacy matters, lies circulate concerning bitcoin, which our brave news outlets often claim is used by criminals and terrorists.

It is of the essence that you do not parrot this claim without careful consideration, and I would back up this first with the reminder that criminals and terrorists *actually prefer cash* and that there are many further uses that blockchain technology can be put to other than cryptocurrency.

On top of that, it is often said that bitcoin is untraceable and therefore attractive to criminals, but this is equally false. Recent examples include an article in the *New York Times* about Republican candidate Rand Paul accepting bitcoin, which describes the currency as 'essentially untraceable' (9th April 2015), followed by *The Guardian* the day after which reiterated this, in what appeared to be an effort to smear the senator.

Calling bitcoin untraceable, however, is tantamount to scaremongering, because bitcoin, by its nature is inherently traceable. The scaremongering that is going on in the consumer technology industry is unwarranted because the blockchain could be monitored by legal authorities, who would be able to extract details of users from it, a fact made hugely simpler if a person of interest exchanges bitcoin for fiat currency, at which point their identity will become obvious.

What this likely indicates is an unwillingness to adapt on the part of governments and industries that could be affected by the popularity of bitcoin. As such, however, the idea that criminals using bitcoin can get away with their exploits without being caught is nonsense, especially when cash is actually harder to trace.

The pause in the implementation of bitcoin then is not because it is criminal but because it is still being tested and because governments and banking industries have not found a way to maximise it to their advantage. You can be sure that if profit could be made from bitcoin simply for the sake of profit, that we would see it adopted everywhere. I would imagine therefore that in the coming decades, attempts will be made to outlaw bitcoin, but as with any good technology – as with the Internet and the printing press before it – the blockchain will remain, simply because it is so good.

'Banks, as they exist now, are obsolete and will not exist as we know them in 10 years,' argued finance and technology entrepreneur Reggie Middleton in 2015. It is a sentiment felt by many, including John McAfee, the founder of the security group McAfee. 'You can't stop things like bitcoin,' he says. 'It will be everywhere and the world will have to readjust. World governments will have to readjust' (CTVNEWS, 28th August 2013).

In future, the decentralised nature of blockchain

technology will be put to many uses. We've discussed the problems faced by the music industry, but these are already being addressed by blockchain technologists. Services like London-based Aurovine already link each play of a musical track to a cryptocurrency payment. This works because a confirmation of who played which track and on which device can be encrypted and logged (and therefore proved) on a blockchain – and a payment can be authorised with no possibility of fraud. The beauty of this system – which could also be applied to webpage views, or e-book downloads, or other media – is that a payment of the equivalent of something like £0.00001 would be expensive for a traditional online payment service to process, but would have no fee at all using a blockchain.

Blockchain technology also allows contracts to be drawn up and put into place. Smart contracts as they are called, are self-executing agreements that automatically release payments once their conditions are met. As these smart contracts rely on data for proof of performance they can resolve disputes without the need for lawyers, and because they use the blockchain, smart contracts are immune to fraud, are tamper proof and are even unaffected by court issued injunctions.

Better yet – not only do smart contracts cut out the need for banks and lawyers, they are actually *more* effective because in the case of traditional contracts, a bank, lawyer, company or any other entity can hold up a transaction indefinitely, even when all agreed conditions have been met. However, a smart contract is operated in such a way that so long as it exists, nothing can hinder its operation, because no single party controls it.

It's also been suggested that blockchain technology can simplify and strengthen supply chains, so it could for example be used to guarantee the origin of food that we purchase, and supply an almost limitless amount of other services. The most terrifying of all for Big Brother however, is the prospect that a blockchain could be used to decentralise governance.

A company called Bitnation is pioneering this idea and offering victims of the world's refugee crisis digital IDs and bitcoin-based credit cards which can be used to receive funds from family members or friends without bank accounts. This works because a blockchain is a shared public ledger, and so can be employed to cryptographically prove a person's identity through family relations, like a sort of international notary public. Bitnation works by generating a barcode that can be used with a mobile app to request a bitcoin credit card, which can be used throughout Europe and the UK without a bank account.

This same process would allow blockchain technology to run a public voting service, whereby people could vote in a completely anonymous and secure manner. There are numerous ways this could be done, but simply put, the blockchain could issue a token to each voter which would be active over a certain time, and would be sent back when the vote was over. There is already an organisation called Counterparty established which believes the exact same distributed and anonymous ledger of votes could be used by everybody. A country could use the same blockchain to vote for a leader, just as a reality TV show could vote for a winner, while a primary school class could similarly use it to vote for their class representative.

The principle would be the same in each case – everyone would be able to see how many anonymised votes had been cast and which issue or person they were cast for.

There may in fact be no reason at all to battle the GCHQ and the NSA, because they already have information on who we are, and so in the case of voting for national or international issues, we could work with them to take down the house of cards, and build a house of glass in which we could watch verifiable but anonymised votes being cast on any issue or in any election. The website bitcongress.org has already proposed such a use for the blockchain in which every person can potentially have complete access to the legislative process.

As of 2016, governments began to take an interest in blockchain technology, with the UK's chief scientific advisor publishing a report asserting that blockchains could be used to track any kind of asset, physical or electronic, as well as monitoring driverless cars. Companies like Stampery offer IP protection via a blockchain, allowing lawyers to certify documents without court fees.

'If the NSA had the blockchain in the heart of its system,' said Stampery co-founder and CTO Luis Ivan Cuende, 'it would have been able to follow Edward Snowden's trail and identify exactly which files he'd accessed and stolen. Snowden was able to access files, then, and as administrator, remove his details. The blockchain would have prevented that – it's immutable' (*Wired*, 23rd November 2016).

As with other promising innovations, Internet hero and tech giant Kim Dotcom has also got designs on the blockchain, and he has proposed nothing short of a new Internet that uses it. Such an Internet he argues, would be immune to mass surveillance because it would not be based on IP addresses. The idea behind Kim Dotcom's MegaNet – the name he suggests for this new internet – would be that we could use the idle bandwidth and storage capacity of the world's billions of devices to carry the service. 'MegaNet won't rely exclusively on mobile networks,' he explained, 'but the more powerful phones become the more data and traffic they will carry' (*International Business Times*, 17th February 2015). The idea that spreading an internet service across the devices owned by its users would mean that no one person or corporation would have an intact copy of any particular file.

This idea, which also underpins BitTorrent's Project Maelstrom, would involve the creation of an Internet powered by people which would solve some of the more pressing concerns regarding the current model. It would also – alarmingly for some – be truly free of censorship, because if a service provider can't identify where web traffic originates, then it can't suppress it.

These are just some of the innovations that are in the process, in some cases, of being criminalised by governments who feel they are losing control, encouraged and sometimes financially supported by corporations, who likewise feel they are losing their grip on long-established markets.

Once there was the television, the radio, the newspapers and the cinema, and large-scale media was effectively one-way traffic. But that has changed.

Now we must ask who the real infobandits are – those who are using their ability and imagination to build systems for the benefit of the world – or those who are caught trying to censor, hinder, stop or criminalise them.

And while we're working out the answer to that question, here's one final hack that you may not have thought of. While the hero of this book, Buckminster Emptier, is working hard to have their data trail amount to nil so that the collection agencies of the present and future are fooled, what if we took the opposite tack, and began to create more data than was necessary? That is, what if we foiled the system by creating large amounts of false data? If, as researcher Emma Stamm states, 'our bodies are now data farms' (*2600*, Autumn 2017) then creating meaningless data might somehow obfuscate the processes at work here. If you are looking for a small object example of this, have a look online and try and guess how many Facebook accounts I have. All my Facebook accounts are called Peter Burnett, all have my image, and all of these accounts have many real and false friends, although only one of them can be, and is 'the real me'.

> A timely example involves the social media 'check-in' ... Speculation from Facebook users who 'checked-in' at Standing Rock, North Dakota in the Fall of 2016 alleged that the website may have complied with legal authorities to reveal possible involvement in the defense of land against government seizure. As a countertactic, Facebook users across the world who supported the defense 'checked-in' to Standing Rock, an action designed to problematize the process of discerning which users were actually in Standing Rock as opposed to those simply on Facebook in another part of the world, legally publicizing their support. This is an exemplary use of obfuscation principles.
>
> (Emma Stamm, *2600*, Autumn 2017)

CONCLUSION

Immediately after he was sworn in as president of the United States on 20th January 2017, Donald Trump began U-turning on his promises. One U-turn that upset many of his own supporters on the libertarian right was his change in attitude to WikiLeaks.

In fact, the Donald had as recently as the previous October been found tweeting 'I love WikiLeaks!', although this seemed, in the cold light of his victory, a rather convenient and empty forgery, one of those vile inaccuracies that liar-politicians use to land-grab votes.

The U-turn was followed by statements made by US Attorney General Jeff Sessions in April 2017, to the effect that arresting Julian Assange was now their priority. The story is so familiar – as I have said before, the US administration is unhealthily, and repetitively obsessed with Julian Assange, and see him as their greatest enemy. Sessions said: 'We are going to step up our effort and already are stepping up our efforts on all leaks. This is a matter that's gone beyond anything I'm aware of' (*The Guardian,* 21st April 2017).

The passion and preoccupation with Assange and electronic leaks has dominated US security policy since the cables and intelligence of 2010 when regimes were toppled and people of the Middle East rose and expressed themselves, mirrored by the Occupy movement elsewhere. At the time, Emmanuel Goldstein wrote:

'Was WikiLeaks the sole cause of all this global mayhem? Certainly not. The ingredients for a tumultuous reaction were already in existence, albeit dormant from so many years of inattention. All it took was a little official confirmation' (*2600*, Spring 2011).

What is not so transparent is how WikiLeaks is directly concerned with the dismantling of power, and this is the reason why it gives Washington so many sleepless nights and why Donald Trump will pursue it with more vigour than any other administration has previously tried. The thinking behind WikiLeaks is recognisable in Julian Assange's pre-2007 blog, iq.org, on which he collected thoughts, poetic essays and other items of interest.

The blog carries as its header a quote from anarchist Gustav Landauer:

> The State is a condition, a certain relationship between human beings, a mode of behaviour; we destroy it by contracting other relationships, by behaving differently toward one another... We are the state, and we shall continue to be the state until we have created the institutions that form a real community and society of men.

As well as the leaked and otherwise hidden documents that it handles, there is a much deeper message resonating in every WikiLeaks story that concerns privacy, truth and corruption. 'The hacker world,' according to Emmanuel Goldstein (above), 'has always long been all about exposing the truth in its various flavours.' The wider implications of the survival of a group like WikiLeaks are a world in which centralised political power is at an end, and a democracy in which information is free.

This is the public front of the USA's war on privacy, and in playing tough with Julian Assange, they hope to silence future whistle-blowers, journalists and other concerned parties. The obsession with leaked secrets and whistle-blowers is telling insofar as it indicates an administration with many, many secrets.

Curiously, when the Swedish prosecutor's investigations of sexual assault against Assange ceased in May 2017, the world's media outnumbered Assange's supporters when he stood on the balcony of the Ecuadorian embassy and addressed us. Julian Assange was by no means out of trouble that day, and his fate is still unclear – less clear than ever perhaps given the priority he had become with the new American administration in 2017.

> Today is an important victory for me and for the UN's human rights system but it by no means erases the years of detention without charge in prison, under house arrest and almost five years here in this embassy without sunlight, seven years without charge while my children grew up without me. And that is not something I can forget, it is not something I can forgive.
> (Julian Assange, May 2017)

To this Assange added: 'While today is an important victory and an important vindication, the road is far from over, the proper war is just commencing.'

At the time of writing, then, Julian Assange has indicated that he will remain inside the Ecuadorian embassy, and that he'll be trying to establish dialogue with British and US officials. His belief is that the US will seek to extradite and then arrest him in connection with WikiLeaks' publication of classified US documents. Assange's position is that the US should recognise his First Amendment rights as a journalist.

As for ourselves, we are a further front in the war and our enemies are harder to observe. A new funding opportunity document issued in 2016 by the US Department of Defence's Office of Naval Research offered a glimpse into proposals concerning how mining social media can provide insight on people's real thoughts, emotions and beliefs, and thereby facilitate predictions of behaviour. (Insurge Intelligence, 1st February 2016).

What I take this to mean is that the same type of US military and federal security contractors which interested Barrett Brown are being offered the chance to win contracts for a new branch of intelligence that will mine social media accounts to predict, among other things, how you will behave when you get angry at the government. Similar pre-crime models are already in action. An unknown number of police authorities for example work with a software called BEWARE which analyses social media activity, property records, and the records of friends, family and associates – among other data – to assign what they call a 'threat-score' to each person they potentially encounter.

How long will it be then, do you think, before somebody is killed by a police official on the grounds that their threat-score indicated that if they were not stopped, then they were going to commit a violent act?

The answer to this and other questions will be uncovered if we permit a wider debate about what kind of government we desire, and the kind of Internet we would like to have.

Battle lines are not drawn on the scale of left and right, but are generational. 'I grew up not just thinking about the Internet, but I grew up in the Internet,' said Edward Snowden – and he speaks for many. It's for this reason that he agrees with Tim Berners-Lee that a Magna Carta for the Internet might be a good idea. However grand it may sound, this Magna Carta for the Internet could allow people to claim their own cyberspace[14] as a form of shared property, and a place safe from basic abuses and criminality. What they envisage is a digital bill of rights that could be tailored to each country or territory – a statement of principles Tim Berners-Lee hopes would be supported by public institutions, government officials and corporations. 'These issues have crept up on us,' said Berners-Lee. 'Our rights are being infringed more and

14 Cyberspace: A society with a fully digital presence in which members of the society contribute to the constant flow of information and interact with one another through digital means. This society exists within many protocols, most famously HTTP, but other protocols as well. (Definition by Daelphinux, *2600*, Summer 2017)

more on every side, and the danger is that we get used to it' (*The Guardian*, 12.03.2014).

Edward Snowden saw a significantly disturbing amount of anti-privacy activity while working in the intelligence community and became aware that there was too much being done in secret without the public's knowledge and consent. One of the more surprising aspects of Edward Snowden's work showed that even the people's representatives in government were not aware of what was happening – and all of this bothered him enough to act.

Following his flight to Hong Kong, Snowden argued that he would not have been able to go to Congress, because there were no legal protections for an intelligence contractor, and he felt there was a risk that he and his data could have been buried without the public knowing about it, so he went to the press. He believes we don't need to give up our privacy to have good government, nor give up our liberty to have security, and many agree with him that the ends (preventing a crime) do not justify the means (violating the rights of the millions whose private records are unconstitutionally seized and analysed).

I would assert that we feel instinctively vulnerable when strangers snoop on our private activities. We immediately change our speech when we aren't anonymous, because surveillance is control, and control is power. The 'I've got nothing to hide' argument hides the implication that privacy is bad because you are in fact hiding something, and this is why search warrants were devised and warrant law came into being as a result of the eighteenth-century boom in the discussion of human rights. Evidence and probable cause are what underpin such warrants, and it is only in authoritarian regimes where police can intrude upon people without having to provide justification or secure court permission to do so.

We have lost the war on privacy and have no option but to trust that the government will do the right thing. We must also trust the corporations who provide us with the technology to use the Internet and this is a battle in its own right. Republicans in the US Congress in March 2017 voted to reverse a FCC privacy rule that opened the door for Internet service providers to sell customer data, although there appears to be no credible reason for this being in the interest of anyone at all. This amounts to the selling of user's web history, once more valuable data, and yet the only people who seem to want it are the people who are going to make lots of money from it. 'Incidentally,' writes *The Verge* (29th March 2017) 'these people and their companies routinely give lots of money to members of Congress,' and figures from federal election data compiled by the National Institute on Money in State Politics (at followthemoney.org) show this to be true, with millions in donations flowing to over 250 politicians in the Senate and the House of Representatives. This change of heart regarding the commercialisation of our data has even got a name – a privacy fire sale. In Britain the Investigatory Powers Bill has now passed and essentially removes UK citizens' rights to privacy. The Bill will force Internet service providers to store a record of our web browsing activity, and an extended and frankly criminal roll of officials will be able to access those records. It also allows our security services to hack devices, and legitimises their own collection of our data in bulk.

In the meantime, Julian Assange has not been charged with any crime in any country. Four prosecutors are currently trying to charge him under the Espionage Act of 1917 before a closed Grand Jury in Virginia, in the United States, but even with the Swedish investigation dropped, none of the persecution has lessened, and in seeking to understand why it may have stepped up again, there is an old quote from the man himself that seems apt: 'The more secretive or unjust an organization is, the more leaks induce fear and paranoia in its leadership and planning coterie' (iq.org, 31st December 2006).

It is in the nature of conclusions to be logical – and yet on the evidence of these pages it could be argued that the only way to stay safe from overzealous government and corporate surveillance is to have neither government nor protected corporations. It is either that or follow the tricky path taken by hacker Buckminster Emptier and cut ourselves off entirely.

It also seems tempting to offer a like it or lump it solution: so long as there are states, there will be war, and so long as there is war, there will be enemies, and so long as there are enemies, there is a need for spies.

However, the maxim that power corrupts would seem to be true and this is why activists tend to favour systems that lean towards transparency. Many of the issues concerning privacy and security could have been addressed by the use of full encryption at the outset of the Internet, and it is now up to us to request and ensure that security be our next great infrastructural change. Free speech does not of course mean saying whatever you like, and so for example, UK and US courts would agree that speech cannot be used as a threat of violence. Similarly, our social contract with the state and each other means that we have to forfeit some amount of a right to privacy. The debate that remains concerns how much a functional society requires the forfeit of these rights for the benefit of all.

The Internet is a perfect tool for the free flow of data and we are as guilty in sharing it as the spies are for collecting it. The good news is that tools are available for the first time which will allow transparency, privacy, security and a few of the other benefits we read about. It will all be down to the direction we take for our next leap forward. Through Internet technology people can speak their minds in a new way – even when governments seek to silence them – and even though data can be collected and controlled, speech and art cannot. Every day I think more about how our privacy is pressed flat in the name of security – face recognition equipment as standard, surveillance of our online activities, scrutinised financial transactions, widespread wiretaps, video cameras on every street, invasive airport screening – and add to that what is sometimes called 'preference' information about our shopping, credit card usage, and deep personal information posted on social networks.

The Internet was the creation of the American academic and military establishment, and it has since its creation being corporatised, democratised and commodified. The Internet has subsequently become very cheap to use and everybody is involved in it with the easiest form of publishing being social media. There is no locality to the Internet and so expansion for any company can seem limitless, as it has proved to be in the cases of the large players such as Google and Amazon Web Services. The uncontrolled populism that this has created is now deemed a threat by both governments and corporations. In the case of governments, this popularism can lead to people and ideas that are not widely accepted becoming accepted, and it has even let some rank outsiders win important elections.

When it comes to corporations, we are now seeing controls being put in place to throttle the free flow of information. In April 2017, Julian Assange reported: 'In response to this outbreak of popularism, Google and Facebook have both formally announced that they are going to introduce a system to be used explicitly in the French election to stop what they see as fake news – while every day, large news organisations pump out fake news, either in the detail or in the headline.' (youtube. com, 31st March 2017).

What Assange is referring to here are value judge-ments, which are fair enough when it comes to reportage itself, but are not constructive when they are used for reasons of censorship.

The governments of the world will not stop at that, and neither will the data industries who aggregate and sell us and our data to one another.

The questions regarding privacy have now been laid out, and it is up to us to assess that corporatisation, democratisation and commodification in light of them. The rebels who have led the way in asking questions and advocating for privacy rights are heroes to me, and yet virtually all of them have been criminalised.

If their work is suppressed, will I become the tar-get instead? Will you?

ACKNOWLEDGEMENTS

Most thanks go to Arlene Addison for loving support in this and other work. Arlene, you have contributed so much to this book – that even includes the title, thank you.

I would like to thank researcher Hannah Henthorn for excellent work collecting, collating and verifying information regarding British and EU privacy legislation, I owe her a great deal. I would also like to thank Dr Todd Swift and Sarah Burk for editorial support and encouragement, as well as Anthony Russell, for permission to use his own outstanding research.

Thanks also go to Karen Lancaster, all my colleagues at and supporters of Free Barrett Brown, and all at the Electronic Frontier Foundation. Author's royalties for the first printing of this book will go towards helping the EFF with their work.

REFERENCES

Specific references and quotations are itemised through-out the text by indicating the publication and the date of the source material.

Articles consulted include:

'Hacked Off', *The Economist*, 28th May 2016

'French MPs Vote to Extend State of Emergency After Paris Terror', 19th November 2015

'Remember Why We Have the Fourth Amendment', The Brennan Center For Justice, 25th November 2016

'Surveillance for the masses: The political and legal land-scape of the UK Investigatory Powers Bill', Burkhard Schafer, Datenschutz und Datensicherheit, (2016), Vol 9, pp 592-597

Books consulted include:

Public Parts: How Sharing in the Digital Age Improves the Way We Work and Live, Jeff Jarvis, Simon and Schuster, 2011

The Information Society Reader, Edited by Frank Webster, Routledge, 2004

Presidents and Civil Liberties from Wilson to Obama: A Story of Poor Custodians by Samuel Walker, Cambridge University Press, 2012

Pirate Politics: The New Information Policy Contests by Patrick Burkart, MIT Press, 2014

Deep Shift; Technology Tipping Points and Societal Impact, World Economic Forum, 2015

YouTube Channels consulted include:
The Forum Network channel of the WGBH
TED Talks
Free Domain Radio
Pirate Party UK

SQUINT
BOOKS

DAVID MASCIOTRA **BARACK OBAMA – INVISIBLE MAN**

OLIVER JONES **DONALD TRUMP – THE RHETORIC**

W STEPHEN GILBERT **JEREMY CORBYN – ACCIDENTAL HERO**

WWW.EYEWEARPUBLISHING.COM